The Funniest Science Jokes In The Universe!

Never date an astronomer. They're star craving mad!

Archaeologist: A guy whose life lies in ruins.

Evolution: God's way of issuing upgrades.

The Hubble Space telescope has captured an image of two galaxies colliding. It's so detailed you can see lawyers rushing to the scene.

These and hundreds more jokes on every discipline await you in this uproarious volume! Be the laugh of the lab with the greatest science joke book in the universe!

The Science Fictionary!

Science Fictionary

The Best Science Jokes

In the Universe

By James Buffington

Word Play

Absolute zero: The lowest grade you can get.

Asymmetry: Where you bury dead people.

Argon: The state north of California.

Activation energy: The useful quantity of energy available in one cup of coffee.

Alternate universe: Where your socks go when the tunnel out of your dryer.

Antidote: A brief, amusing story.

Asteroid belt: Used to keep the asteroids in place.

Astronomer: A skyentist . .

Astronomer: One who watches and catalogues nocturnal emissions.

Astronomical unit: Refers to the cost of an Air Force toilet.

Aurora Borealis: An exotic dancer in Nome, Alaska.

Avalanche: A mountain getting it's rocks off.

Bacteria: Back door to the cafeteria.

Beta radiation: Radiation in the testing phase.

Betelgeuse: The stuff you squeegee off the windshield of your car.

Biological Science: A contradiction in terms.

Biology: The study of shopping.

Black hole: That sump in your basement.

Black holes : What you get in black socks.

Brazilian: A really big number.

Brownian motion: A jogging girl scout.

Bucky Balls: A beloved cartoon character.

Bunsen Burner: A device invented by Robert Bunsen for brewing coffee in the   laboratory.

Bunsen Burner: The only safe method of Bunsen disposal.

Bermuda Triangles: Diet breakfast cereal that makes pounds disappear without a trace.

Butyl: An unpleasant-sounding word denoting an unpleasant-smelling alcohol.

Calculus of residues: Wow to clean up a bathtub ring.

Chandrasekar Limit: Three beers.

Chemical: A substance that:
  1. An organic chemist turns into a foul odor;
  2. An analytical chemist turns into a procedure;
  3. A physical chemist turns into a straight line;
  4. A biochemist turns into a helix;
  5. A chemical engineer turns into a profit.

Chemical Engineering: The practice of doing for a profit what an organic chemist does for fun.

Clinical Testing: The use of humans as guinea pigs.

Clock drive: Refers to the street beneath Big Ben.

Coma: Italian, multi toothed device for arranging ones hair.

Cold fusion: Frozen energy drink.

Compound: To make worse, as in: 1) A fracture; 2) the mutual adulteration of two or more elements.

Computer Resources: The major item of any budget, allowing for the acquisition of any capital equipment that is obsolete before the purchase request is released.

Commutator: A student who drives to school.

Conic Section: Funny paper.

Corona: An officer who enquires into the manner of violent death.

Cosine: The opposite of stop sign.

Critical mass: A gaggle of film reviewers.

Cusp: To use profane language.

Critical mass: A gaggle of film reviewers.

Dark matter: A morbid subject.

Diagnostic: One who believes 2 may neither be proved nor disproved.

Drake equation: method for calculating mallards.

Eigen Function: The use to which an eigen is put.

Einstein: One beer.

Einstein-Rosen bridge: a bridge in New York.

Electron: What the US did in 1980 and 1984.

Electron: A voting machine.

Ether Oar: Small positioning thruster used by NASA.

Evaporation Allowance: The volume of alcohol that the graduate students can drink in a year's time.

Exhaustive Methylation: A marathon event in which the participants methylate until they drop from exhaustion.

Fehling solution: Method for reducing size of a chemistry class.

Ferric: Ironic.

Fission: What atoms do for fun. .

Flux: Past participle of "to flex."

Gaseous prominence: Barack Obama.

Geologist: Fault finder.

Geology: Rock it science.

Gluons: Little stickers featuring cartoon characters you find all over.

Gram: To review for examinations.

Graph: Principle item of bovine diet.

Gravitational Lens: The new contact your kid drops through an open grate.

Gravity: a heartless bitch.

Ground State: Coffee before brewing.

Hard Water: Stronger than soft water.

Harmonic function: A concert .

Hermitian operator: Recluse surgeon.

Hertz: Prime ingredient in donuts.

Higgs Field: A baseball stadium.

Humbug: noisy wire tap.

Hypered Film: is when you really need to brush your teeth.

Hyperspace : Where you park at the superstore.

Hypotenuse: Animal like rhinoceros but with no horn on nose.

Inorganic Chemistry: That which is left over after the organic, analytical, and physical chemists get through picking over the periodic table.

Interpolate: Breeding a statistician with a clergyman to produce the much sought "honest statistician".

Kilogram: What scientists send instead of postcards.

Large Hadron Collider: One ring to rule them all.

Lecithin: Fat Lite.

Lassie: The dog star.

Life: A series of Schroedinger's boxes.

Light Pollution: A few beer cans in the yard.

Light Year: The opposite of a heavy year.

Light Year: A period of time when you don't have enough cash.

Maksutov: A wine bottle filled with gasoline and thrown at tanks.

Monomer: One mer.

Marginal ray: A ray of doubtful origin.

Max Plank: The biggest board you can find.

Membrane: The opposite of forgettin'.

Meson: Member of secret sub-atomic society.

Meteorites: Pending legislation permitting meteors to traverse U.S. air space.

Mu Meson: Bovine member of above society.

Multiverse: A really long poem.

Neutrino: Opposite of an old trino.

Neutrino: A high energy breakfast bar.

Normal: an underachiever.

Nucleotide: Effect of moon on an atom.

P-brane: A liberal arts major.

Paradigm: Twenty cents.

Penumbra: Something you need during a rain shower or when you need to write a note

Perihelion: A guy who sang "That's Amore" in the 1950s.

Periscope: Close approach to instrument used for viewing periwinkles.

Pharmacology: The use of rabbits and dogs as guinea pigs.

PHD: Piled high and deeper.

PHD: Pretty horny dude.

Photosphere: A snapshot of a beach ball.

Physical Chemistry: The pitiful attempt to apply $y=mx+b$ to everything in the universe.

Pilot Plant: A modest facility used for confirming design errors before they are built into a costly, full-scale production facility.

Plank Constant: A board of uniform dimensions.

Planetarium: A place for raising vegetables.

Pluto : Mickey's sidekick.

Polygon: An ex-parrot.

Polymer: Many mers.

Poynting Vector: A redundant term since all vectors point.

Prelims: An obligatory ritual practiced by graduate students just before the granting of a Ph.D.

Preparation A: Used to relieve the pain and suffering of asteroids.

Proton: A fat hooker.

Publish or Perish: The imposed, involuntary choice between fame and oblivion, neither of which is handled gracefully by most faculty members.

Purple Passion: A deadly libation prepared by mixing equal volumes of grape juice and lab alcohol.

Quantum Mechanics: A crew kept on the payroll to repair quantums, which decay frequently to the ground state.

Quark: Sound made by duck with speech impediment.

Radioisotope: Used to listen to the stars.

Rarification: First indication a species may be endangered.

Refractor: Then Vito breaks your leg for the second time.

Relativity: A gathering of family members.

Research: That which I do for the benefit of humanity, you do for the money, he does to hog all the glory.

Sagan: The international unit of humility.

Satellite: What you put on your horse if you're riding at night.

Schmidt-Cassegrain: A German meal made with rice.

Scientific Method: The widely held philosophy that a theory can never be proved, only disproved, and that all attempts to explain anything are therefore futile.

Semiconductor: part-time musician.

SI: acronym for "Systeme Infernelle".

Solar Carona: Warm Mexican beer.

Solar Wind: What your fat uncle had after Thanksgiving dinner.

Spectra: Female ghost.

Spectrophotometry: A long word used mainly to intimidate freshman nonmajors.

Spectroscope: A disgusting-looking instrument used by medical specialists to probe and examine the spectrum.

Sphere: A long pointed weapon.

Spin Operator: Owner of a ferris wheel.

Square roots: Used to keep squares in place.

Standard Model: A four door sedan.

Standard Normal Deviates: A comparison group of sociopaths who were formally normal people.

Star Chart: Predicts the future.

Star Party: A Hollywood bash.

Statistics: A bunch of numbers looking for a fight.

String Theory: used to master yo-yos.

Superconductor: Leonerd Bernstein.

Suture Self: Home medical kit.

Tachyon: A sticky particle.

Telescope: Device designed to ensure a profitable flu season.

Time: Nature's way of keeping everything from happening at once.

Time Travel: Throwing the alarm clock at the wall.

Titration: A limit set at the cathouse.

Torus: a four door sedan.

Toxicology: The wholesale slaughter of white rats bred especially for that purpose.

Umbra: Something you need during a rain shower.

Uncertainty Principle: Strategy for guessing on multiple choice tests.

Uranus: An anatomical feature rather than a planet.

Walkers Quark Bars: sweetness and 'charm.

WIMPS: Scrawny beach bums.

Wormhole: Where you get night crawlers.

Zodiacal Light: A low alcohol beer.

Anthropology Jokes

A Jewish anthropologist, Benny Steinfeld, was working in the desert near Israel when he happened upon an odd looking vase. After cleaning it he pried open the lid and was astonished when a genie sprang from the container and granted him 3 wishes. Steinfeld wished for enormous wealth, huge land holdings and a bevy of beautiful wives. All wishes were granted, but on one condition. Never again in his life could the anthropologist get a haircut or shave. To do so would mean instant imprisonment in the same urn in which the genie had been imprisoned. All went well during the first few years of his lavish lifestyle, but his beard and long hair became more and more of a problem. One day, during a moment of weakness and desperation he ran to the bathroom, grabbed some scissors and began cutting off his beard. Immediately his fortunes vanished, and he found himself trapped in the urn lying in the desert sand. The moral of this story? "A Benny shaved is a Benny urned."

What is the usual composition of a typical Dogon family? Mother, father, two children and a French Anthropologist!

Why was Darwin a bad man?
Because he was an Evilutionist!

An anthropologist was filling in an application for grant money after spending an entire day in the field, so he was pretty tired. Under family name, he wrote "Hominidae"

An anthropologist was assigned to Borneo, where he hired a guide with a canoe to take him up the river to the remote site where he would make his collections. At noon on the second day of travel up the river they began to hear drums.
"What are those drums?" asked the anthropologist, knowing they were in cannibal country.   The guide turned to him

and said "No worry. Drums OK, but very bad when they stop."

They both went ghostly pale when the drums suddenly stopped. The guide crouched in the belly of the canoe and covered his ears.

"Do as I do! Very important!" intoned the guide with great urgency. "Why? What does this mean?" asked the panicked anthropologist.

"Drums stop! Next come guitar solo!"

A skeptical anthropologist was cataloging South American folk remedies with the assistance of a tribal brujo who indicated that the leaves of a particular fern were a sure cure for any case of constipation. When the anthropologist expressed his doubts, the brujo looked him in the eye and said, "Let me tell you, with fronds like these, who needs enemas?"

In our final class of Anthropology, the revered old professor lectured about race.

He lectured that in his opinion there was no such thing as race. That every living person was their own individual race. And that the only thing we should care about is the human race. A perplexed student stood up and asked the professor: "How do we classify people then?".

The professor then calmly replied: If you must classify someone, there is only one thing you should classify them by. The student yelled: "What's that?"

The professor replied: Whether or not that person is an asshole!

Two anthropologists fly to the south sea islands to study the natives. They go to two adjacent islands and set to work. A few months later one of them takes a canoe over to the other island to see how his colleague is doing. When he gets there, he finds the other anthropologist standing among a group of natives.

"Greetings! How is it going?" says the visiting anthropologist.

"Wonderful!" says the other, "I have discovered an important fact about the local language! Watch!". He points at a palm tree and says "What is that?".
The natives, in unison, say "Umbalo-gong!".
He then points at a rock and says "And that?".
The natives again intone "Umbalo-gong!".
"You see!", says the beaming anthropologist, "They use the SAME word for 'rock' and for 'palm tree'!".
"That is truly amazing!" says the astonished visiting anthropologist, "On the other island, the same word means 'Fuck you'!".

Anthropologist: "Are there any bats in this cave?"
Native guide: "There were, but don't worry, the snakes ate all of them."

A native guide was giving a talk to a group of anthropology students about hiking in grizzly bear territory: "Most bear encounters occur when hikers, being extra quiet along the trails in hopes of viewing wildlife, accidentally stumble into bears. The resulting surprise can be catastrophic." To avoid this, he suggested that each hiker wear tiny bells on their clothing to warn the bears of their presence. "Also," he said further, "be especially cautious when you see signs of bears in the area, especially when you see bear droppings."
One student asked, "How do you identify bear droppings?"
"Oh, that's easy," the guide explained, "it's the ones with all the tiny bells in them!
An anthropologist in the deepest Amazon suddenly finds himself surrounded by a bloodthirsty group of natives. Upon surveying his situation, he says quietly to himself, "I'm screwed."
There is a ray of light from the sky and a voice booms out: "No you are NOT screwed. Pick up that stone in front of you and bash the head of the chief."
So the anthropologist picks up the stone and proceeds to bash in the head of the chief. He is breathing heavily while standing above the lifeless body. Surrounding him are the

100 native warriors with a look of shock on their faces.
The voice booms out again: "Okay.......NOW you're screwed!"
Sumo wrestling: Survival of the fattest.

If Darwin was right, you will probably figure it out in a few million years.

One day the anthropologist noticed that the orang-utan was reading two books - the Bible and Darwin's The Origin of Species. In surprise he asked the ape, "Why are you reading both those books"?
"Well," said the orang-utang, "I just wanted to know if I was my brother's keeper or my keeper's brother."

The theory of evolution was greatly objected to because it made man think.

'I love fools' experiments; I am always making them.' Charles Darwin

A primatologist and a baboon are walking down the street. They meet a second primatologist who says, "Hey, what are you doing with that ape?"
The first primatologist says, "Excuse me, you should know a baboon is not an ape. He's a type of old world monkey."
The second one says, "Yes, I know that, but I wasn't talking to you."

Two anthropologists are hiking through the jungle when they turn a corner and come face to face with a big lion. The lion looks at them and then crouches, about to charge.
Without hesitation, one guy whips off his back pack, pulls out a pair of running shoes, and sits down to replace his hiking boots with the running shoes.
The other guy looks at him and says "Are you crazy? You can't outrun a lion!"
The first guy, as he finishes lacing his running shoes, stands

up and replies: "I don't have to run faster than the lion. I just have to run faster than you."

An unemployed anthropologist got a new job at the zoo. They offered him to dress up in a gorilla's skin and pretend to be a gorilla so people will keep coming to the zoo.
On his first day on the job, the guy puts on the skin and goes into the cage. The people all cheer to see him. He starts really putting on a show, jumping around, beating his chest and roaring.
During one acrobatic attempt, he loses his balance and crashes through some safety netting, landing square in the middle of the lion cage! As he lies there stunned, the lion roars. He's terrified and starts screaming, "Help, Help!"
The lion races over to him, places his paws on his chest and hisses, "Shut up or we'll both lose our jobs!"

Evolution is God's way of issuing upgrades.

Evolutionism: The speciocity of speciation!

When evolution is outlawed only outlaws will evolve.

A young anthropologist got fired from his first real wildlife job. Upon his return home, his parents asked him what happened.
"You know what a crew boss is?" he asked. "The one who stands around and watches everyone else work."
"What's that got to do with it?" they asked.
"Well, he just got jealous of me," the young anthropologist explained. "Everyone thought I was the crew boss."

A little girl asked her mother, "How did the human race come about?"
The mother answered, "God made Adam and Eve; they had children and, so all mankind was made."

A few days later, the little girl asked her father the same question. The father answered, "Many years ago there were monkeys, and we developed from them."

The confused girl returns to her mother and says, "Mom, how is it possible that you told me that the human race was created by God , and dad says we developed from monkeys?"

The mother answers, "Well, dear, it is very simple. I told you about the origin of my side of the family, and your father told you about his side."

Why did the chicken cross the road?
Darwin:
A1: It was the logical next step after coming down from the trees.
A2: The fittest chickens cross the road.
A3: Chickens, over great periods of time, have been naturally selected in such a way that they are now genetically dispositioned to cross roads.

Why did the chicken cross the road?
Evolutionist: Pure chance.
Evolutionist: Only the fittest chickens survive crossing the road.
Creationist: God created the chicken on the other side of the road. There is no proof it ever was on this side.

Why did the dinosaur cross the road?
Chickens hadn't evolved yet.

If evolution is true then why is it so easy for women to make monkeys out of men?

If creationism is true and we are made in God's image then how do you explain politicians?

A anthropologist walks into a bar with his pet monkey. He orders a drink and while he's drinking, the monkey starts jumping all over the place. The monkey grabs some olives off the bar and eats them, then grabs some sliced limes and eats them, then jumps up on the pool table, grabs the cue ball, sticks it in his mouth and swallows it whole.

The bartender screams at the anthropologist, "Did you see what your monkey just did?"

The anthropologist says, "No, what?"

"He just ate the cue ball off my pool table - whole!" says the bartender.

"Yeah, that doesn't surprise me," replies the patron. "He eats everything in sight, the little twerp. I'll pay for the cue ball and stuff." He finishes his drink, pays his bill, and leaves. Two weeks later he's in the bar again, and he has his monkey with him. He orders a drink and the monkey starts running around the bar again.

While the anthropologist is drinking, the monkey finds a maraschino cherry on the bar. He grabs it, sticks it up his butt, pulls it out, and eats it. The bartender is disgusted. "Did you see what your monkey did now?"

"Now what?" asks the anthropologist.

"Well, he stuck a maraschino cherry up his butt, then pulled it out and ate it!" says the barkeeper.

"Yeah, that doesn't surprise me," replies the patron. "He still eats everything in sight, but ever since he ate that damn cue ball he measures everything first!"

Then there was the anthropologist who was studying a cannibal tribe and broke a taboo.

He ended up in hot water.

A anthropologist had been working on a remote research project in the Amazon jungle. Upon his return to the States, he came down with a terrible illness. After his health had deteriorated, his wife took him to a doctor who specialized in strange jungle diseases. The doctor gave him a complete examination and a series of tests. After receiving the results of the tests, the doctor called the wife into his office alone. He told the young anthropologist's wife, "Your husband is suffering from a very severe disease, combined with horrible stress. If you don't do the following, your husband will surely die. Each morning, fix him a healthy breakfast. Be pleasant, and make sure he is in a good mood. For lunch make him a nutritious meal. For dinner prepare an especially nice meal for him. Don't burden him with chores, and generally do anything he asks. Don't discuss your problems with him, as it will only make his stress worse. And most importantly, make love with your husband several times a week and satisfy his every whim. " If you can do this for the next 10 months or so, I think your husband will regain his health completely. Otherwise.......well... He'll probably die"

On the way home, the husband asked his wife. "What did the doctor say?"

She replied. "Honey.....he says you're probably going to die."

Two cannibals were having their dinner. One said to the other "I don't like anthropologists."

The other one said, "Well, put him to one side and just eat the vegetables."

Cannibals capture three anthropologists. The men are told that they will be skinned and eaten and then their skin will be used to make canoes. Then they are each given a final request. The first man asks to be killed as quickly and painlessly as possible. His request is granted, and they poison him. The second man asks for paper and a pen so that he can write a farewell letter to his family. This request is granted, and after he writes his letter, they kill him saving his skin for their canoes. Now it is the third man's turn. He asks for a fork. The cannibals are confused, but it is his final request, so they give him a fork. As soon as he has the fork he begins stabbing himself all over and shouts, "To hell with your canoes!"

A man is captured by cannibals, every day they poke him with spears and use his blood to wash down their food .Finally the guy calls the chief over and says, "Hey, you can kill me or you can eat me, but I m tired of getting stuck for drinks!"

A cannibal chief was just about to stew his latest victim for dinner when the man protested, "You can't eat me ? I'm an editor for Anthropology Review!"
"Well," said the cannibal, "soon you'll be a editor in chief."

Two anthropologists in Africa get apprehended by a tribe of very hostile cannibals who put them in a large pot of water, build a huge fire under it, and leave them there. A few minutes later, one of the anthropologists starts to laugh uncontrollably. The other anthropologisr can't believe it! He says, "What's wrong with you? We're being boiled alive! They're gonna eat us! What could possibly be funny at a time like this?"
The other anthropologist says, "I just peed in the soup."

How many evolutionists does it take to change a light bulb?
Only one, but it takes eight million years.

Archaeology Jokes

An archeologist is a person whose career lies in ruins!

How do you ring an Egyptian doorbell?
Tutankhamun (Toot and come in!)

Who invented the pen?
The Inkas.

An archaeologist was digging in the Negev Desert in Israel and came upon a casket containing a mummy. After examining it, he called the curator of a prestigious natural history museum.
"I've just discovered a 3,000 year old mummy of a man who died of heart failure!" the excited scientist exclaimed.
To which the curator replied, "Bring him in. We'll check it out."
A week later, the amazed curator called the archaeologist.
"You were right about the mummy's age and cause of death. How in the world did you know?"
"Easy. There was a piece of paper in his hand that said, '10,000 Shekels on Goliath'."

Most mothers tell their daughters to marry doctors...
I told mine to marry an archeologist because the older she gets, the more interested he will be in her.

"A British archeologist has found globs of flavored tar that was chewed and spat out by a prehistoric man," says Jenny Church. "It's the first fossil evidence of Major League Baseball."

A team of archaeologists was excavating in Israel when they came upon a cave. Written on the wall of the cave were the following symbols in order of appearance.

1. A woman

2. A donkey
3. A shovel
4. A fish
5. A Star of David

They decided that this was a unique find and the writings were at least more than three thousand years old. They chopped out the piece of stone and had it brought to the museum where archaeologists from all over the world came to study the ancient symbols.

They held a huge meeting after months of conferences to discuss what they could agree was the meaning of the markings. The President of their society stood up and pointed at the first drawing and said:

"This looks like a woman. We can judge that this race was family oriented and held women in high esteem. "

"You can also tell they were intelligent, as the next symbol resembles a donkey, so, they were smart enough to have animals help them till the soil. The next drawing looks like a shovel of some sort, which means they even had tools to help them."

"Even further proof of their high intelligence is the fish which means that if they had a famine hit the earth, whereby the food didn't grow, they would take to the sea for food."

"The last symbol appears to be the Star of David which means they were evidently Hebrews."

The audience applauded enthusiastically and the President smiled and said, "I'm glad to see that you are all in full agreement with our interpretations."

Suddenly a little old man stood up in the back of the room and said, "I object to every word. The explanation of what the writings say is quite simple. First of all, everyone knows that Hebrews don't read from left to right, but from right to left... Now, look again...It now says:

"'Holy Mackerel, Dig The Ass On That Woman!'"

How do you embarrass an archeologist?
Give him a used tampon and ask him which period it came from.

The young archaeology said, "They put me in the same tent with old Doctor Perkins. He snores all night, passes wind, takes a bath once a month, and talks non-stop about back when he studied passenger pigeons. He's so damn old, I think he was a lackey for Charles Darwin. He generally just makes my life Hell. We had a big fight about it and they split us up for a month"

The older archaeologist said, "That should make you happy."
The young archaeologist sadly shook his head and said, "Not when the month is up today!"

Did you hear about the angry mummy?
He flipped his lid.

What do you get in a 5-star pyramid?
Tomb with a view.

Two archaeologists were excavating a tomb in Egypt.
Arch.1: I just found another tomb of a mummified pharoah!
Arch 2: Are you serious?
Arch 1: No bones about it!

What do you call a very, very, very, very, very old joke?
Pre-hysterical!

Did you hear the one about the archaeologist that was found napping on the job?
Answer: Apparently he was stoned.

How many druids does it take to change a light bulb?
Sixteen. One to change the light bulb and fifteen to realign the stones.

After a hard day's excavation, an Egyptologist had a pain in her lower back.
It didn't last long though, she was ok after she saw a cairopractitioner!

Why are archaeologists greedy?
We want archaic... and eat it too!

Why did the archaeology student cry?
Because he lost his mummy.

What happened when the pottery specialist lost her job?
She got fired.

What does B.C. stand for?
Before computers.

Which Aztec king was the best wrestler?
Montesumo.

Archaeologists are the worst gossips.
They're always digging up dirt on people.

Archaeologists are always unfaithful.
They'll date anybody.

'Did you hear the joke about the archaeologist who had two skulls of Cleopatra, one as a young girl, and the other as a grown woman?'

After having dug to a depth of 10 meters last year, New York scientists found traces of copper wire dating back 100 years and came to the conclusion that their ancestors already had a telephone network more than 100 years ago.
Not to be outdone by the New Yorkers, in the weeks that followed, California scientists dug to a depth of 20 meters, and shortly after, headlines in the LA Times newspaper read: 'California archaeologists have found traces of 200 year old copper wire and have concluded that their ancestors already had an advanced high-tech communications network a hundred years earlier than the New Yorkers.'

One week later the 'Moose Jaw Times Herald', a local newspaper in Saskatchewan reported the following:
'After digging as deep as 30 meters in sagebrush fields near Moose Jaw, Ole Johnson, a self-taught archaeologist, reported that he found absolutely nothing. Ole has therefore concluded that 300 years ago, Saskatchewan had already gone wireless.'

A mummy covered in chocolate and nuts has just been discovered in Egypt!!!
Archaeologists believe it may be Pharaoh Roche.

Do mummies enjoy being mummies?
Of corpse!

What did the sign In front of the Ancient Egyptian funeral home say?
 Satisfaction guaranteed or double your MUMMY back!

A tourist is traveling with a guide through one of the thickest jungles in Latin America, when he comes across an ancient Mayan temple. The tourist is entranced by the temple, and asks the guide for details. To this, the guide states that archaeologists are carrying out excavations, and still finding great treasures. The tourist then queries how old the temple is."This temple is 2503 years old", replies the guide.
Impressed at this accurate dating, he inquires as to how he gave this precise figure.
"Easy", replies the guide, "the archaeologists said the temple was 2500 years old, and that was three years ago."

What do you call a friendly dead Egyptian?
A Chummy Mummy.

Two gorgeous blonde archaeologists were in the field one fine summer day. While following a trail, they came across a pair of tracks. "Look! a pair of tracks" The first blonde said while pointing to the ground. "Those are deer tracks," the other blonde replied. "Oh no," she said to the first, "Those are definitely moose tracks." With this, they began to argue. In fact, they were still arguing when the train hit them.

An archaeology crew leader has several crews, each consisting of two grad students. The crews camped and worked in the woods and he made his rounds to visit each pair every few days. One particular crew, Sarah and Jim, were not getting nearly as much work accomplished as the others, so he suspected that they might be up to some funny business. The following day, he paid them a visit."Is anything funny going on here?" he asked.
"What do you mean by that?" the pair asked back.
"I mean, you're not getting much fieldwork done. Are you two, you know, maybe doing something you're not supposed to do?"
"Absolutely not!" the Jim replied. " We are strictly co-workers"
"Oh yes," the Sarah replied, " We hike all day, record our data, return back, and fall asleep exhausted."That's right!" Jim replied, "and me in my tent, and she in hers!"
The crew supervisor spent the remainder of the day in the field with the pair. He left the field early, returned to camp, retrieved his Jeep and left the area.
The following day grad students had lost their $1000 GPS unit. They searched high and low, but could not find it. It had simply disappeared from their camp. After a few frantic days, they suspected that the crew leader had taken it. It was the only plausible explanation. That evening, they called him on the 2-way radio, and politely asked whether he may have inadvertently taken the unit.
"As a matter of fact, I did take it the day I came up to see if you two were sleeping together. After realizing I had accidentally taken it with me from the field, I placed it in Sarah's sleeping bag where she would be sure to find it!"

What is a Mummy's favorite type of music?
Wrap!

Archaeologists take sedimental journeys.

How many archaeologists does it take to change a light bulb?
Three. One to change it while the other two argue about how
old the old one is.

According to archaeologists, for millions of years
Neanderthal man was not fully erect. That's pretty easy to
understand considering how ugly Neanderthal woman were.

Anyone who fails to see the evolutionary link between man
and ape has never used the restroom at a Walmart.

Are you an archaeologist? Because I've got a bone in my
pants that I'd like you to date it.

What has been dug cannot be undug

All archaeology research is groundbreaking.

Archaeologists do it in the dirt. Forensic Archaeologists do it
in the dirt with dead bodies!

How many archaeologists does it take to change a light bulb?
Answer: Are you kidding?! Why would we let them do that?!
The broken bulb is a national treasure, pointing to our rich,
rich history and culture. No, we would rather build a shrine
there, and charge admission to see the 'ancient luminosity
device'. Hmmm, maybe we could even sell little figurines.

What do men and mummies have in common?
Answer: They both like being tied up.

What do women and trowels have in common?
Answer: They both like it dirty.

The greatest contribution archaeology has ever provided to society is the simple fact that everybody is destined to become a feature.

Today's disaster is tomorrow's archaeology.

I sort of thought I wanted to be an archaeologist. But my father suggested I go to a cocktail party full of archaeologists first. I did. He's a very wise man.

Astronomy Jokes

It is reported that Copernicus' parents said the following to him at the age of twelve: "Copernicus, young man, when are you going to come to terms with the fact that the world does not revolve around you."

Is the name of an over-the-counter product used to relieve the pain and suffering of asteroids Preparation A?

"Why does the Moon orbit the Earth?"
"To get to the other side."

Black holes are what you get in black socks

An English major at a university was taking an astronomy course to satisfy the science requirement. During the last lecture of the semester, the professor spoke about some of the more exotic objects in the universe including black holes. Despite his teacher's enthusiasm, the student showed no interest, as was the case for all his astronomy classes during the semester. When the bell rang, the student turned to his friend and said, "The prof says that black holes are interesting, but I think they suck."

An astronomy major had a part time job working in the university's off-campus housing office. One day, a fellow student, upon entering the office in thought about the morning lecture, asked, "What is an astronomical unit?"
 To which the astronomy major replied, "One helluva big apartment."

Teacher: "How long does it take the Earth to rotate about its axis?"
Student: "The Earth makes a resolution once every 24

hours."

Teacher: "That's wishful thinking."

How many astronomers does it take to screw in a lightbulb?
Answer: Astronomers have no time for screwing!

What's a light-year?
One third less calories than a regular year.

Light-Dog-Year = 1/7 light-years.

So, Sirius, the "dog star", is about 58.8 light-dog-years away.
And the star Wolf 359 is about 53.9 light-dog-years away.

Why didn't the dog star laugh at the joke?
It was too Sirius

What kind of cartoons do Martians watch?
Loonertunes

How does the solar system holds up its pants?
With an asteroid belt.

If a meteorite hits a planet, what do we call the ones that miss?
Meteorwrongs

What kind of songs do the planets like to sing?
Nep-tunes.

What did Saturn say to Jupiter when he asked if he could call him?
Don't call me, I'll give you a ring.

How does the man in the moon cut his hair?
Eclipse it.

A spiral galaxy walks into a pub. The landlord says "Sorry mate, you're barred".

"In awe I watched the waxing moon ride across the zenith of the heavens like an amber chariot towards the ebony void of infinite space, wherein the tethered belts of Jupiter and Mars hang forever festooned in their orbital majesty. And as I looked at all this I thought: 'I must put a roof on the bedroom'."

A Black Hole is a tunnel at the end of light

The Hubble Space telescope has captured an image of two galaxies colliding. It's so detailed you can see lawyers rushing to the scene.

How many light bulbs does it take to screw up an astronomer?

I was up all night wondering where the Sun had gone... then it dawned on me

After his first meal on the Moon, the 22nd century astronaut said the food was good but the restaurant lacked atmosphere

What did the astronaut cook for lunch?
An unidentified frying object.

A n astronomer walks into a bar and says to the bartender, "Gimme a Mexican beer."
Instead of handing him a beer, though, the bartender starts shouting "Okay, everybody out! Right now! Out you go!" and herds everyone out into thestreet.
The astronomer shakes his head sadly. "Dang," he remarks, "I should've seen that Corona mass ejection coming."

Why did the chicken cross the road
Carl Sagan:
There are billions and billions and billions of such chickens, crossing roads just lie this one, all across the universe.

Why did the chicken cross the road?
Hubble:
There are two possibilities: One that the distance between the chicken and the side of the road that it was on before it crossed is expanding, and the other, that the distance is contracting, and will collapse on itself.

Why didn't the sun go to college?
Because it already had a million degrees.

Do the stars and planets control our lives?
 No; the IRS maybe, but not the stars and planets.

Heard about the new Hubble cocktail, it's expensive and when you drink it, everything looks fuzzy ...

An astronomer is on an expedition to Darkest Africa to observe a total eclipse of the sun, which will only be observable there, when he's captured by cannibals. The eclipse is due the next day around noon. To gain his freedom he plans to pose as a god and threaten to extinguish the sun if he's not released, but the timing has to be just right. So, in the few words of the cannibals' primitive tongue that he knows, he asks his guard what time they plan to kill him.
The guard's answer is, "Tradition has it that captives are to be killed when the sun reaches the highest point in the sky on the day after their capture so that they may be cooked and ready to be served for the evening meal".
"Great", the astronomer replies.
The guard continues, though, "But because everyone's so excited about it, in your case we're going to wait until after the eclipse."

Where do astronauts keep their sandwiches?
In a launch box.

How do you organize a space party?
You planet.

It is estimated that 3.71 X 10^10 "first-star-tonight" wishes have been wasted on Venus.

"Sir! I have just spent the last 6 hrs at our telescope and have made an astonishing discovery! However, there is good news, and bad news!"
The old astronomer, naturally, asks: "What is the good news?"
"I have just discovered a new star, that has just appeared, and is only 14 light years away from our own!", replied the young astronomer.
"My God, that's fantastic, that's wonderful, amazing, etc. What bad news could there possibly be about that?" The old astronomer queried.
The young astronomer replies, "Sir, it's BLUE!"

How many radio astronomers does it take to change a light bulb?
 None. They are not interested in that short wave stuff.

What do you call an alien with three eyes?
An aliiien!!

Two astronomers. One is looking through the telescope and the other is standing next to him.
Astronomer No. 1: Hey! I can see Uranus!
Astronomer No. 2: That telescope must be a funny shape!

After intensive investigation on both the Soviet and US parts, spokespersons from both space agencies have determined the cause for the accident which has placed the station and its resident personnel in jeopardy. In terse statements at a recent press conference, Soviet and US space agency spokespersons said Thursday We have concluded joint investigations concerning this potentially tragic accident and each nations' team, separately, has arrived at identical conclusions for this incident. The accident was caused by one

thing and one thing only...
OBJECTS IN MIR ARE CLOSER THAN THEY APPEAR

How do you get a baby astronaut to sleep?
You rocket.

When is the moon the heaviest?
When it's full.

Did you hear the one about the claustrophobic astronaut? He needed some space.

How is the astronomer doing?
Things are looking up.

Astronomy divided by stupidity equals astrology.

Why is an astronaut like a football player?
They both want touchdowns.

Star light, star bright
First star I see tonight
I wish I may, I wish I might.
Oh, Darn! It's just a satellite

What did the shooting star say to the atmosphere?
"You burn me up!"

Does it snow on Pluto?
No, not if Mickey lets him inside!

From the remarks of Sherlock Holmes:
"It's a capital mistake to theorize before you have all the evidence."
It follows that astronomers are bad detectives.

Freshmen in the general-science class in Middle School were studying astronomy.

"What do we call a group of stars that makes an imaginary picture in the sky?" the teacher asked.
"A consternation," one student replied.

Why did the planet get kicked out of college?
"He kept mooning the class."

A day without sunshine is like night

Gravity brings me down.

What's an astronomer's favorite candy?
Milky Way!

Q. How do astronomers see in the dark?
A. They use standard candles!

Sirius, the dog star, is drawing closer to earth at a rate of nine miles a second. Someday we could be in Sirius trouble.

What do two black holes talk to each other about?
Dark matters.

Whenever anyone asks me what my hobbies are, I always say I enjoy watching heavenly bodies.

Scientists studying the sun have a flare for research.

How many astronomers does it take to change a light bulb?
None! Astronomers aren't afraid of the dark.

I do not feel obliged to believe that the same God who has endowed us with sense, reason, and intellect has intended us to forgo their use.
– Galileo Galilei

Astronomy puns? This could get messy. Or messier.

What's the most popular snack on Mars?
Marshmallows.

"If there are no aliens, why can't NASA show us pictures of them not being?"

Stellar Evolution: The transformation of Demi Moore from a Stripper in Striptease to a Navy SEAL
Two blondes staring at the Moon.
1st blonde "Which do you think is closest, the Moon or California?.
2nd blonde "Duh, can you see California from here!"

What would you do if you saw a space man ?
I would park in it man.

July 20th, 1999 marked the 30th Anniversary of the lunar landing. To commemorate the event, Neil Armstrong, "Buzz" Aldrin, and Michael Collins arrived at Cape Canaveral together in a limousine. Neil and Buzz joined the day's festivities, and Michael was left sitting in the car.

Jupiter came down to Earth one day and decided to help these two criminals to rob a bank. Anyway, to make a long story short, they got caught and the three of them found themselves in court. The judge sentenced the two earthlings to fifteen years, and Jupiter was a bit shocked when he was sentenced to ten years.
"But your honour" said Jupiter, "I didn't even take part in the robbery!"
"Yes" said the judge. "But you helped them ... Planet!".

They were the first to attempt to colonize Mars. They knew it would be difficult , but they were determined to succeed. They had landed with grass seeds to plant and embryos of horse, sheep and cattle. But the grass wouldn't grow, and none of the calves survived. The horses and sheep were doing well, but there not enough animals to meet their needs. So they sent a message to earth asking for more sheep and horses and a replacement for the cattle and grass. They particularly wanted an animal that could be used as meat in place of beef.

Earth radioed back asking if venison would be satisfactory and the colonists replied it was.

Finally a space shuttle arrived with the needed supplies. The bill of lading was rushed to the leader of the colony who then spoke to his consul "We got everything we asked for," he shouted. . . . "They sent mare zygotes and doe zygotes and little lambs and ivy."

Living on Earth may be expensive, but it includes an annual free trip around the Sun.

I'm not saying this is a legitimate reason to major in astrophysics, but the fact is, once you attain light speed it's basically goodbye college loan officers forever.

"I'm quite fond of astronomy," Tom said nebulously.

How far can you see on a clear day?
 93 Million miles...From here to the Sun.

 Why is it called Mooning when you're actually showing Uranus?

I heard they're changing the name if Uranus to stop all these cheap jokes. It will be re-named Urectum!

Two astrophysicists are discussing their research in a bar one evening when a drunk who has been sitting and listening in at the next seat turns and says, in a very worried voice, "What was that you just said?"
"We were discussion stellar evolution, and I said to my colleague here that the Sun would run out of nuclear fuel and turn into a red giant star in about 5 billion years, possibly melting the Earth."

"Whew!" says the drunk, "You really had me worried. I thought you said 5 million."

When do astronauts have lunch? At Launch Time.

How do you know that Saturn is married more than once?
Because he has lots of rings.

How did the astronaut serve dinner in outer space?
On flying saucers.
Scientists have shown that the moon is moving away at a tiny, although measurable distance from the earth every year. If you do the math, you can calculate that 85 million years ago the moon was orbiting the earth at a distance of about 35 feet from the earth's surface.
This would explain the death of the dinosaurs...the tallest ones, anyway.

Why did the astronomer order a double hamburger?
He wanted a meteor burger!

Why did the sun get straight A's?
Because it was so bright!

How is the moon like a dollar?
It has four quarters!

What do you call a space magician ?
A flying sorcerer !

"It's a good thing the guy in charge of naming galaxies was into chocolate bars and not Chinese food. Otherwise, the Milky Way might have been named Moo Goo Gui Pan,

Teacher: Tomorrow there will be a lecture on Sun. Everyone must attend it.
Mary: No madam! I will not be able to attend it.
Teacher: Why?
Mary: My mother will not allow me to go so far!

A theologian and an astronomer were talking together one day. The astronomer said that after reading widely in the field of religion, he had concluded that all religion could be summed up in a single phrase. "Do unto others as you would have them do unto you," he said, with a bit of smugness, knowing that his field is so much more complex.
After a brief pause, the theologian replied that after reading widely in the area of astronomy he had concluded that all of it could be summed up in a single phrase also.
"Oh, and what is that?" the astronaut inquired.
"Twinkle, twinkle, little star; how I wonder what you are!"

There is just one thing I can promise you about the outer-space program: your tax dollar will go farther.
– Wernher von Braun.

It is not conclusive yet, but the NASA believes the Mars Curiosity has found proof of life on Mars. The CD player was stolen.

My Other Car is a Saturn

What kind of star wears sunglasses?
A movie star.

Cosmologists Do It with a Big Bang
Sherlock Holmes and Dr. Watson go on a camping trip, set up their tent, and fall asleep. Some hours later, Holmes wakes his faithful friend. "Watson, look up at the sky and tell me what you see."
Watson replies, "I see millions of stars."
"What does that tell you?"
Watson ponders a minute. "Astronomically speaking, it tells me that there are millions of galaxies and potentially billions of planets. Astrologically, it tells me that Saturn is in Leo. Time wise, it appears to be approximately a quarter past three. Meteorologically, it seems we will have a beautiful day tomorrow. What does it tell you?"

Holmes is silent for a moment, then speaks. "Watson, you idiot, someone has stolen our tent."

Did you hear about the astronomer with no name?
Astrononamer.

When NASA was preparing for the Apollo Project, it took the astronauts to a Navajo reservation in Arizona for training.
One day, a Navajo elder and his son came across the space crew walking among the rocks.
The elder, who spoke only Navajo, asked a question.
His son translated for the NASA people: "What are these guys in the big suits doing?"
One of the astronauts said that they were practicing for a trip to the moon.
When his son relayed this comment the Navajo elder got all excited and asked if it would be possible to give to the astronauts a message to deliver to the moon.
Recognizing a promotional opportunity when he saw one, a NASA official accompanying the astronauts said, "Why certainly!" and told an underling to get a tape recorder.
The Navajo elder's comments into the microphone were brief. The NASA official asked the son if he would translate what his father had said.
The son listened to the recording and laughed uproariously. But he refused to translate. So the NASA people took the tape to a nearby Navajo village and played it for other members of the tribe. They too laughed long and loudly but also refused to translate the elder's message to the moon.
Finally, an official government translator was summoned. After he finally stopped laughing
the translator relayed the message:
"Watch out for these ********. They have come to steal your land."

Whatever the missing mass of the universe is, I hope it's not in cockroaches.

The universe is simple; it's the explanation that's complex.

Only in the USA will you find people who think the moon landing was fake and wrestling is real.

Everything in the Universe is rushing away from you at ever-increasing speed. . . . Want to try some new breath mints?

Did you hear that NASA recently launched a bunch of cows into low Earth orbit?
They called it the Herd Shot 'Round The World!

Astronomy is much too Sirius to make jokes about.

Big news! Scientists have decoded the first message from an alien civilization What did it say?
Simply send 6 x 10^50 atoms of hydrogen to the star system at the top of the list, cross off that star system, then put your star system at the bottom of the list and send it to 100 other star systems. Within one-tenth of a galactic rotation you will receive enough hydrogen to power your civilization until entropy reaches its maximum!
IT REALLY WORKS!

Why don't astronauts get hungry after being blasted into space?
Because they've just had a big launch.

Earth First! We'll strip mine the other planets later.

Two astronauts were in a space ship circling high above the earth. One had to go on a space walk while the other stayed inside. When the space walker tried to get back inside the space ship, he discovered that the cabin door was locked, so he knocked. There was no answer. He knocked again, louder this time. There was still no answer. Finally he hammered at the door as hard as he could and heard a voice from inside the space ship saying, 'Who's there?'

Why don't astronauts get hungry after being blasted into space?
Because they've just had a big launch.

Why don't astronauts keep their jobs very long?
Because as soon as they start they get fired.

There were three volunteers that were trying out for a new NASA experiment on sending people to different planets.
They called in the first volunteer and asked her a question. "If you could go to any planet, what planet would you want to go to and why?"
After pondering the question she answered, "I would like to go to Mars because it seems so interesting with all the recent news about possible extra terrestrial life on the planet."
They said, "Well okay, thank you." And told her that they would get back to her."
The next volunteer entered the room and the NASA people asked him the same question. In reply he said, "I would like to go to Saturn to see all of its rings."
They also said, "thank you", and that they would get back to him.
The third volunteer, a blonde, entered the room and they asked him the same question that they had asked the other two volunteers. "What planet would you like to go to?"
He thought for a while and replied, "I would like to go to the sun."
The people from NASA chuckled, as the sun isn't a planet, but they decided to play along with this idiot, and asked "Why? Don't you know that if you went to the sun you would burn to death?"
The blonde smirked and crossed his arms confidently across his chest. "Are you guys dumb? I'd go at night of course!"

If an athlete gets athlete's foot, what does an astronaut get?
Missile toe.

Some people can tell what time it is by looking at the sun. But I have never been able to make out the numbers.

The beguiling ideas about science quoted here were gleaned from essays, exams, and classroom discussions. Most were from 5th and 6th graders. They illustrate Mark Twain's contention that the 'most interesting information comes from children, for they tell all they know and then stop.

What is one horsepower?
One horsepower is the amount of energy it takes to drag a horse 500 feet in one second.

You can listen to thunder after lightning and tell how close you came to getting hit. If you don't hear it, you got hit, so never mind.

Talc is found on rocks and on babies.

How many ears does Spock have?
Three: a left ear, a right ear, and a final frontier.

The law of gravity says no fair jumping up without coming back down.

When they broke open molecules, they found they were only stuffed with atoms. But when they broke open atoms, they found them stuffed with explosions.

When people run around and around in circles we say they are crazy. When planets do it we say they are orbiting.

Most books now say our sun is a star. But it still knows how to change back into a sun in the daytime.

Which astronaut wears the biggest helmet?
The one with the biggest head.

I just found germs on my chocolate bar.
I guess that proves there is life on Mars.

Astronomers are star craving mad.

What is an astronomer? A night watchman with a college education.

Where do astronauts leave their spaceships?
At parking meteors.

What do you call a loony spaceman ?
An astronut !

If you've seen one class 1a supernova you've seen them all.

Fight aging. Travel at light speed.

The sun is lighter than the earth. That's why it rises every morning.

What do I have in common with neutrinos?
Uh, we're both constantly penetrating your mom.

My husband is an astronomer. I asked what he was working on. He said he was looking for the center of the universe. I said, "Here I am!"

On July 8, 1947, witnesses claim a spaceship with five aliens aboard crashed on a sheep-and-cattle ranch outside Roswell, an incident they say has been covered up by the military. March 31, 1948, nine months after that day, Al Gore was born.
That clears up a lot of things.

Feathers are light.
The sun gives off light.
Therefore, the sun gives off feathers.

Astronauts do it above the atmosphere.
Astronomers do it all night.
Astronomers do it cosmologically.
Astronomers do it elliptically.
Astronomers do it hyperbolically.
Astronomers do it in voids.
Astronomers do it in X-ways.
Astronomers do it orbitally.
Astronomers do it parabolically.
Astronomers do it spectroscopically.
Astronomers do it meteorically.
Astronomers do it on mountain tops.
Astronomers do it in clusters.
Astronomers do it telescopically.
Astronomers do it under the stars.
Astronomers do it with Uranus.
Astronomers do it with young stars.
Astronomers do it universally.
Astronomers do it variably.
Astronomers do it while gazing at Uranus.
Astronomers do it in nebulae.
Astronomers do it in the dark.
Astronomers do it with lenses.
Astronomers do it with long tubes.
Astronomers do it with mirrors.
Astronomers do it with sextants.
Astronomers do it with stars.

Yo mama's so fat, she doesn't paint her toenails, they are red-shifted.

Yo mama's so fat, tightening her belt causes her to drop below her Schwarzschild Radius.

Your mama's so fat that if she moved past a black hole at a high velocity she'd create a closed, timelike, curve.

Things Astronomers Say that Sound Dirty, but Really Aren't . .
1) "Exactly how long is your tube?"
2) "I need a friend to help me grind this thing..."
3) "I want to get in a little naked-eye action."
4) "I want to look at Uranus?"
5) "You need a bigger unit so you can go deeper..."
6) "What's the best way to mount a Short-Tube?"
7) Reasons why smaller apertures are better...
8) Are you going to shoot the Virgin tonight?
9) She looked in awe as it rose higher and higher.
10) "Mine is bigger than yours"
11) "Who says size doesn't matter?"
12) "We do it in the dark"
13)"We sometimes do it all night long"
14 EYEGASMS!
15) "I use shower caps over the end of my 6 and 10 inch...,
you will need the extra large size for your 12.5 inch."
16) "Do you have your angle of the dangle correct?"
17) "I enjoy viewing heavenly bodies through my
telescope...especially during showers"
18) "I love going deep ...."
19) "The deeper the better"
20) "Bigger almost always performs better"

You Know You Are A Redneck Astronomer If...

(1)The most important part of your instrumentation is the pickup truck.

(2) You have a Tasco refractor up on blocks in the front yard.

(3) Your observing site would be perfect if it weren't for the alligators.

(4) You carry a shotgun to deal with skunks, raccoons, and streetlights.

(5) you have a board with holes on the side of the DOB mount fit beer cans (the eyepieces already have a little box they came in -duh!).

(6) A cup holder by the eyepiece has a partial beer to balance different eyepieces. (Amazing how many need replacing as they get too light.)

(7) You will fight that SOB trying to find WWV when it was already on a perfectly good country station.

(8) You tell all the guys at the star party about that neat dang drinking fountain next to the toilet in them big fancy hotels.

(9) The counterweight on your Dob doubles as a spit can.

(10) You've used lard to slick those declination bearings.

(11) Others at the star party complain about the smoke when you barbecue spam.

(12) You start to giggle when you tell your buddies that you have a 16-incher.

(13) You ever wonder what your granny's truss has to do with building a telescope.

(14) You've ever tried to use your granny's truss to build a telescope.

(15) You nostalgically refer to Canis Major as Old Duke.

(16) You look at pictures of the Flame Nebula (or the Rosette) to get in the mood.

(17) You lie and tell your buddies the next morning that your red eyes are from drinking and partying rather than stargazing.

The Ten Commandments for Amateur Astronomers

1. Thou shalt not love thy telescope more than thy spouse or thy children; as much as, maybe, but not more.
2. Thou shalt not covet thy neighbor's telescope, unless it exceeds in aperture or electronics twice that of thy wildest dreams.
3. Thou shalt not read "Astronomy" or "Sky & Telescope" on company time, for thine employer makes it possible to continue thine astronomical hobby.
4. Thou shalt have at least two telescopes so as to keep thy spouse interested when the same accompanies thee under the night sky or on eclipse expeditions to strange lands where exotic wild animals doth roam freely.
5. Thou shalt not allow either thy sons or thy daughters to get married during the Holy Days of Starfest.
6. Thou shalt not reveal to thy spouse the true cost of thy telescope collection; only the individual components and that shall be done with great infrequency.
7. Thou shalt not buy thy spouse any lenses, filters, dew shields, maps, charts, or any other necessities for Christmas, anniversaries, or birthdays unless thy spouse needs them for their own telescope.
8. Thou shalt not deceive thy spouse into thinking that ye are taking them for a romantic Saturday night drive when indeed thou art heading for a dark sky site.
9. Thou shalt not store thy telescope in thy living room, dining room, or bedroom, lest thou be sleeping with it full time.
10. Thou shalt have no white light before thee, behind thee, or to the side of thee whilst sharing the night sky with thy fellow stargazers

YOU MIGHT BE AN AMATEUR ASTRONOMER IF:

You think that not getting enough sleep at night is a good thing.

You ask your optometrist about the availability of H-Alpha Sunglasses.

You center your vacation time around the New Moon.

You don't buy a house until you've had a chance to see how dark the neighborhood gets at night.

You build your dream home with a roll-off roof (or optionally, a rotating dome roof).

All the night lights in your house are red.

Somebody asks you where you live and you tell him the latitude and longitude of your house.

Somebody asks where your town is and you pull out a map and show him how to "starhop" from town to town to find it.

You've named your kids and pets after stars or constellations.

A pair of binoculars and a small refractor are always in your trunk, just in case.

Your neighborhood seems to always have more than its share of non-functioning streetlights and porch lights.

You can hand-draw your own star charts down to the 7th magnitude -- from memory!

When you take a new vehicle for a test drive, the first thing you do is run by home to see whether your telescope will fit in the trunk.

During droughts, farmers in your area collect donations to allow you to buy more telescope equipment (to make it rain).

You spend more money per year at your favorite optics store than you do at Wal-Mart.

You plant and trim hedges (especially evergreens) and erect yard art to block nearby lights.

Your friends and colleagues tell just you about the beautiful sky they saw the other night.

You have a propensity for buying toys that glow in the dark.

You rewire your house to 12VDC so that it's compatible.

Your spouse complains about always having to turn the brightness up on the monitor in the morning.

How many astronomers does it take to change a light bulb?

I thought astronomers used standard candles.

Two: one to change the bulb, the other to complain about the light pollution.

Only one, but you have to go to Hawaii to get the really good bulbs.

Three, plus or minus seventy-five.

10^8, because astronomers love really big numbers !

None, they wouldn't change it because it ruins their night vision.

Murphy's Law for Astronomers

Law of Selective Gravitation:
Small items (e.g. locking screws) will land in the place from which they are most difficult to retrieve; heavy items (e.g. counterweights) will land where they cause the most pain and/or damage. (Usually "and".)

Law of Selective Observation:
The next supernova will occur in a galaxy that you observed on the previous clear night.

Law of Selective Declination:
The most interesting astronomical event of the year will occur at a declination that is below the horizon of your observing site.

Law of Selective Vegetation:
The neighbour's tree always migrates to precisely the right place to occult your target object.

Sod's Law (Astronomer's variant of):
A dropped optic will always land surface-side down, unless it is either capped or dropped for the express purpose of proving this law.

Law of Inevitable Shrinkage:
Anything cut to size will be too small.

Law of Temporary Loss:
A lost item will stay lost until it is either replaced or no longer required.

Law of Averted Vision:
The brightest meteor of the night will occur behind

you, visible only to the people to whom you are talking at the time. (This is true for all observers, including those to whom you were talking.)

Lunar Radiation Principle:
Deep Sky observers will find that the clearest nights are around Full Moon, when the lunar radiation is sufficient to drive off the clouds and haze.

Daylight Conundrum:
With the unique exception of total solar eclipses, the year's ten most interesting astronomical events will occur when the Sun is above your horizon, unless it is raining.

Biology Jokes

With friends like you who needs flesh eating bacteria?

Why did the germ cross the microscope?
To get to the other slide.

We just hired a molecular biologist. Man, is he small.

Scientifically, maybe body cells do replace themselves completely in seven years -- but, legally, you're still married.

What do you call the leader of a biology gang?
The nucleus.

Did you hear about the famous microbiologist who traveled in thirty different countries and learned to speak six languages?
He was a man of many cultures.

A fellow accidentally ingested some alpha-L-glucose and discovered that he had no ill effects.
Apparently he was ambidextrose.

A genetic engineering project focused on developing a breed of cattle which are only 6 inches [15 cm] tall.
If the project is successful, members of the research project are hoping to make a fortune selling microchips.

What did one cell say to his sister cell when she stepped in his toe?
Mitosis .

How does Juliet maintain a constant body temperature?
Romeostasis.

If my right leg is the cell wall and my left is the membrane, do you want to be the cytoplasm?

A woman called her husband during the day and asked him to pick up some organic vegetables for that night's dinner on his way home. The husband arrived at the store and began to search all over for organic vegetables before finally asking the produce guy where they were. The produce guy didn't know what he was talking about, so the husband said: "These vegetables are for my wife. Have they been sprayed with poisonous chemicals?" To which the produce guy replied, "No, sir, you will have to do that yourself."

The bad news is that the American Society for the Prevention of Cruelty to Amoebas is shrinking. The good news is that none of the amoebas has lost any of their members.

Once there was a beautiful biologist who loved to work in her vegetable garden, but no matter what she did, she couldn't get her genetically enhanced tomatoes to ripen. Admiring her neighbor's garden, which had beautiful bright red organic tomatoes, she went one day and inquired of him his secret. "It's really quite simple," the old man explained. "Twice each day, in the morning and in the evening, I expose myself in front of the tomatoes and they turn red with embarrassment."
Desperate for the perfect garden, she tried his advice and proceeded to expose herself to her plants twice daily. Two weeks passed and her neighbor stopped by to check her progress. "So," he asked, "any luck with your tomatoes?" "No," she replied excitedly... "but you should see the size of my cucumbers!"
There was a biology student who was studying equilibrium in sea birds with a specific focus on terns. He proposed that

giving measured doses of THC (from, of course, marijuana) and observing their flight patterns would give some insight to the problems of equilibrium in three dimensional space. This proposal being given in a more liberal era, the student got the funding. He filled out mountains of forms, set up a lab with a ready supply of terns, and proceeded on his way.

After a year of diligent work, groveling monthly before the review committee to get his stipend, and living with drugged terns, he completed his study.

With trembling hands, he delivered his 247-page report, complete with charts and graphs, to the review committee. The august body peruses his study, asking penetrating questions and reducing our student to jell-o. Finally, the department head rises. The light reflects off her steel rimmed glasses as she stares down at our student. "There is a lot of good work here," she says. "But we can't accept this report. You have detailed marvelously the effects of THC on terns but you forgot one essential step: you have no control group."

Our student turns pale and says, "You don't mean..."

"Yes. I'm afraid so. You left no tern unstoned."

How did the English major define microtome on his biology exam?
 An itsy bitsy book.

What did the Smooth Endoplasmic Reticulum say the the Rough Endoplasmic Reticulum?
Answer: Is that a ribosome on you or are you happy to see me?

Apparently one day there was a lab where all the students werelearning how to identify various cells. As samples they were using tissue scraped from the inside of the mouth. One girl was having terrible difficulties figuring out what kind of cell she was seeing under her microscope--eventually she called over the teaching assistant to identify it.

He came over, smirked, and exclaimed, loud enough for everyone to hear,
"Oh wow! That's a sperm cell!"
She was somewhat more careful after that experience....

Confucius's once said, "When you breathe, you inspire, and when you do not breathe, you expire."

"How does blood circulate in the human body?"
"I not exactly sure. Does it go down the right leg and up the left?"

"Can you name the three kinds of blood vessels?"
"Yes. Arteries, veins and caterpillars."

"Where is the alimentary canal located?"
"Is it at the border of New York State and Canada?"

The unknown sequences of DNA will decode into copyright notices and patent protections.

A bacteriologist is a man whose conversation always starts with the germ of an idea.

What did one lab rat say to the other?
"I've got my scientist so well trained that every time I push the buzzer, he brings me a snack.

It has been discovered that research causes cancer in laboratory rats.

A biologist is only a lab rat's way of making another lab rat.

The medical student was shocked when he received a failing grade in radiology. Approaching the professor, he demanded to know the reason for the grade.
"You know the self X-ray you took?" asked the professor.
"I do." said the student.

"A fine picture," the professor said,"of your lungs, stomach, and liver."
"If it's a fine picture, then why did you give me an F?" asked the student.
"I had no choice," said the professor. "You didn't put your heart in it."

Teacher: "What is the definition of a protein?'
Student: "A protein is something that is made up of mean old acids."

Teacher: "What kind of tails do opossums have?"
Student: "Reprehensible ones"

Teacher: "What is the spinal column?"
Student: "A long bunch of bones. The head sits on the top and you sit on the bottom."

Two elderly gentlemen were visiting. "I guess you're never too old," the first one boasted. "Why just yesterday a pretty college girl said she'd be interested in dating me. But to be perfectly honest, I don't quite understand it."
"Well," said his friend, "you have to remember that nowadays women are more aggressive. They don't mind being the one to ask."
"No, I don't think it's that." "Well, maybe you remind her of her father."
"No, it's not that either. It's just that she also mentioned something about carbon 14."

How many company biotechnologists does it take to change a light bulb?
Four: one to write the proposal, one to design the bulb-changer, one to design the bulb-fetcher, and one to design the bulb.

How many freelance biotechnologists does it take to change a light bulb?

One; he designs the bulb to crawl up the wall, unscrew the old one and   screw itself in.

New embryological research on salamanders has shown that when the optic nerve is connected to the anus at a very early stage of development, the organism usually develops into an animal with hindsight. Some of the animals show symptoms of tunnel vision.

Two guys, called Joe and Dean, were fishermen. Every day, before dawn, they set out to sea with their crews, coming home late in the evening with their catches of fish. Now, there was one particular area where they would cast their nets, because of a particular type of fish which was to be found there. This was a mutant type of fish which had no hearing apparatus.
These rare fish fetched a high price from the local marine biologists who liked to study them. Now, the area where Joe and Dean caught these fish was very difficult to reach, and involved long hours of sailing through treacherous waters, which Joe didn't like at all. Well, one week, Joe didn't turn up for work at all, and when one of his crew went to Joe's house to find out what was wrong, Joe said, "I don't know what's wrong with me. I'm feeling really tired and lethargic. I have no energy at all."
"Don't worry," said the crewman, "Dean has been putting all his catch of those mutant fish through as yours, so you will still have some money to pay our wages this week."
"Oh, no," said Joe. "That means that I will have to get over this feeling of exhaustion and go out to that awful bit of the sea next week, and all because I OWE DEAN DEAF FISH IN SEA."
(Iodine deficiency)

I was grading exams, and a student referred to the components of a two hybrid screen as "bait" and "pray." There may be some truth to that!

How so you call a member of the financial staff of the faculty of Biology?
A Buy-ologist.

The subtle irony of a neurotoxin like acrylamide is that you are the last one to realize that you should have worn gloves.

As we took notes, out anatomy instructor labored through a lecture on the way nerve cells transmit impulses. "Who can tell me how these cells communicate with one another?" he asked, expecting someone to explain the phenomenon of neurotransmission.
After a few muffled whispers, one student finally spoke up. "With cellular phones?"

Sign on the door of the microbiology lab: 'STAPH ONLY!'"

A biology professor was addressing his class, wanting to see if they'd read the assigned text. He asked Miss Smith to stand. She does.
Professor: Miss Smith, what part of the human body increases ten times when excited?
Miss Smith blushes and hesitates and giggles.
Professor: Miss Smith, please sit down. Miss Jones, please stand and tell me if you know what part of the human body increases ten times when excited.
Miss Jones: Yes, Professor. It's the pupil of the eye.
Professor: Very good. Thank you Miss Jones, you may sit down. Miss Smith, will you please stand again. (She does) I have three things to say to you.
1. You have not done your homework
2. You have a very dirty mind.
3. You're in for a big disappointment.

Two biologists studying caribou in Alaska's back country got a pilot to fly them into the far north to collect some specimens. They were quite successful in their venture and had six big carcasses to take back to their lab. The pilot came back, as arranged, to pick them up. They started loading their gear into the plane, including the six caribou. But the pilot objected and told them, "Those caribou carcasses are too heavy, the plane can only take four of them . You will have to leave two behind." They argued with the pilot, letting him know that the year before, they had also collected six caribou and that pilot had allowed them to put all six animals aboard. This plane was the exact same model and capacity. Reluctantly, the pilot finally permitted them to put all six aboard. But when they attempted to take off and leave the valley, the little plane could not carry the load and they crashed into the wilderness.

Climbing out of the wreckage, one biologist said to the other, "Do you know where we are?"

"I think so," replied the other biologist. I think this is about the same place where we crashed last year!"

Organ transplantation in the future. Brain transplantations are possible between relatives (immunological advantage). Father dies and donates his brain to his daughter. How do you call such a donor father?
You call him Brain-dad.

What do you have upon a request for a mother's identification?
Cardamom.

Did you hear about the biologist who had twins?
 She baptized one and kept the other as a control.

Neural crest: An oral hygiene product for the brain. Use with mental floss.

"Biology is the only science in which multiplication means the same thing as division."

Do molecular biologists wear designer genes?

A trio of biologists were studying fruit flies and attempting to do micro-scopic observations. The first put his scalpel to work under the micro-scope and began to slice. He successfully chopped the wings off.
The second biologist began to work, and with a bit more effort managed to slice off the head from the body. Then the third one went to work, but nothing visible happened.
His two colleagues looked at him in astonishment. "What are you going to cut off?" one of them asked.
His response was:"You said to cut the fly, so this one won't be having children any more!"

The worst part of studying genetic engineering is when your homework eats your dog.

Cloning is for people who enjoy making fools of themselves.

Of course it's possible to produce life in the laboratory.
It just depends on who you are with.

Why didn't the dendrochronologist get married?
All he ever dated was trees!

How did the herpetologist know he would be married soon?
He caught the garter snake.

How do you call eight Rabbits?
One Rabbyte

How do you call a positively charged pussy-cat?
A CATion

How do you call a laboratory in which they use rats as test-animals?
Lab-rat-ory.

What rock band keeps changing their music?
Mutagenesis.

Which biochemicals wash up on beaches?
Nucleotides.

What is a paramecium?
Two Latin mice.

What is the only thing worse than a mecium?
A Paramecium

As what did the antibody go to the Halloween costume party?
As an "immunogoblin"

How do you tell the sex of chromosome?
Pull down it's genes

What did the male stamen say to the female pistil?
I like your "style"

A red blood cell walked into a busy restaurant. The hostess
asked, "Would you like to sit at the bar?"
The red cell answered, "No thanks, I'll just circulate."

Q. What does DNA stand for?
A. National Dyslexics Association.

There was this biologist who was doing some experiments
with frogs. He was measuring just how far frogs could jump.
So he puts a frog on a line and says "Jump frog, jump!". The
frog jumps 2 feet. He writes in his lab book: 'Frog with 4 legs
- jumps 2 feet'.
Next he chops off one of the legs and repeats the experiment.
"Jump frog jump!" he says. The frog manages to jump 1.5
feet. So he writes in his lab book: 'Frog with 3 legs - jumps
1.5 feet'.
He chops off another and the frog only jumps 1 foot. He
writes in his book: 'Frog with 2 legs jumps 1 foot'.
He continues and removes yet another leg. " Jump frog
jump!" and the frog somehow jumps a half of a foot. So he

writes in his lab book again: 'Frog with one leg - jumps 0.5 feet'.

Finally he chops off the last leg. He puts the frog on the line and tells it to jump. "Jump frog, jump!". The frog doesn't move. "Jump frog, jump!!!". Again the frog stays on the line. "Come on frog, jump!". But to no avail.

The biologist finally writes in his book: 'Frog with no legs - goes deaf'

Something tells me that no matter how good a series of experiments on reproductive technologies, the paper written about the work will never be described as seminal.

I think that we should salute the dedicated scientists who spend every waking hour slaving at the bench and in the clinics, working like dogs, neglecting single-mindedly in pursuit of the answer to the causes of Obsessive Compulsive Disorder.

People who go through waves of euphoria can be said to be suffering from PEP-tides.

What do you call a faulty spirometer?
Expired!

What's a biologists definition of a graph
An animal with a long neck.

Biology grows on you.

Eat yogurt and get cultured

How do you make a hormone?
Don't pay her.

A mushroom walks into a bar and the bartender says," sorry we don't serve mushrooms here."
And the mushroom replies, " Why? I'm a Fun-gi?

"Today," said the professor , "I will be lecturing about the liver and spleen."
Up in the gallery, one med student leaned toward the other, "Damn, it there's one thing I can't stand ... it's an organ recital!"

In this modern era, where cloning, hybrid and generic engineering have become household words, few of us remember the true pioneer of genetic experimentation. I am, of course speaking of Dr. Moreau. Not the Dr. Moreau immortalized by H. G. Wells in his famous novel, but the real Pierre Moreau who actually attempted to form new species from unrelated animals. Most of his experiments failed. Most of the documents that survived deal with his attempts to cross a dog and a cat, but none lived more than a few hours after birth. His studies were ridiculed by the French Academy of Science and he died in disgrace not realizing he was a hundred years ahead of his time. He had only a single real success, which occurred when he cloned the chromosomes of the black rhinoceros with the giant panda of China. Only one of this new species, which he called a pandaceros survived beyond infancy but with diligence and care, one did grow to full maturity.
This magnificent animal was over five foot tall and weighed 500 pounds. It had a long soft black and white fur coat and a 18 inch hollow cylindrical horn on its forehead. The horn communicated through a canal with the posterior pharynx, which, unlike the elephant which uses its trunk to breathe, was primary used for feeding. His daily supply of bamboo shoots and berries was placed in the horn and with the use of a plunger-like devise invented by Dr. Moreau, the beast could get its frequent feedings as it desired. It was a loving animal, ideal for a pet, and loved to play with children. Unfortunately, like most hybrids, it was sterile. This made commercial production of pandaceri uneconomical, and the process was never repeated by Dr. Moreau or his disciples.
In 1895, faced with forced closure of his island laboratories,

Moreau sold his only successful hybrid to the Circus de Royal, where it was the premier attraction for two years before its untimely death from pneumonia. Visitors from throughout the world travelled to have an opportunity to pet this wonderful beast. For a few years, the Circus de Royal was the most talked about and visited entertainment center in all of Europe.

Now, one hundred years after the untimely death of the world's only pandaceros, there are few still alive that remember their trips to the circus and the excitement of seeing and petting the magnificent ... furry
with the syringe on the top.

The couple left the gynecologist's office with the wife in tears. They were just told that she could never become pregnant. They would never have the family they both desired so fervently.

Suddenly, a masked man appeared before them. "I think I can help you," he said, handing them a card.

"Why are you masked?" the husband asked.

"Because the government has declared our activities illegal. Go to the address on this card. The doctor will take a scrapping from one of your mouths and culture it. In less than a year, we will have your baby for you."

"This is the answer to our prayers!" the wife exclaimed. Then she turned to thank the stranger but he was gone. "Who was that masked man?"she asked her husband.

He answered, "That was the Clone Arranger"

A botanist was delighted when identified a new breed of garden pest. He had discovered a new lice on leaf.

Peptide: The result of the moon pulling on the Pepsi.

What did one thermophilic bacteriologist say online to another?
"I think you are really hot. Your PCR or mine?"

Where do they send the criminal neurons?
To the chain ganglion.

There are some happy sciences, but others are not so happy.
A case in point concerns embryologists who tend to be a
morose and saddened group than most. No wonder. One of
the first things they learn is that our lives are
ova before they've begun.

In the neurobiology lecture the professor mentioned that
much of the data we were seeing was culled from studies of
leeches. He said, "Now, a lot of you may think leeches are
nasty creatures. The people working with these creatures are
quite fond of them, however. It is also reported that
the leeches often become attached to the researchers."

A seventh grade Biology teacher arranged a demonstration
for his class.
He took two earth worms and in front of the class he did the
following:
He dropped the first worm into a beaker of water where it
dropped to the bottom and wriggled about. He dropped the
second worm into a beaker of Ethyl alcohol and it
immediately shriveled up and died. He asked the class if
anyone knew what this demonstration was intended to show
them.
A boy in the second row immediately shot his arm up and,
when called on said: "You're showing us that if you drink
alcohol, you won't have worms."

Biologists do it with clones.
Molecular biologists do it with hot probes.
Zoologists do it with animals.
Geneticists do it with sick genes.
Geneticists do it Animalistically

A little neurological put down:
You've only got two neurons--and one of them's inhibitory.

Enzymes are things invented by biologists that explain things which otherwise require harder thinking.

What did the femur say to the patella?
I kneed you.

Why do noses run but feet smell?

A frog telephones the Psychic Hotline. His Personal Psychic Advisor tells him, "You are going to meet a beautiful young girl who will want to know everything about you."
The frog is thrilled, "This is great! Will I meet her at a party?"
"No," says his advisor, "in her biology class."

Where do you bury dead people?
Asymmetry

What do football players wear on their heads?
Helminth

What is the reproductive area in South America?
Spermatagoni

Where do hippos go to university?
Hippocampus.

How do you know your dehydrated?
You can hear your red blood cells crenating.

Biologists do it with clones. Botanists do it in the bushes. Zoologists do it with animals.

There once was a snake breeder who had two snakes he was trying to mate. For the life of him, he couldn't get them within two feet of each other. Frustrated, he called up the local zoologist, and explained the situation. She hurried over, picked up the snakes and looked at them. "You know what I would do?" she said. "See that tree over there? Chop it down, chop off a good sized log, split the log in two, and make two tables out of them. Put the tables and the snakes into a cage, and let them go at it."

Well, the breeder thought that this was insane, but having no other options, he tried it. Sure enough, a few days later he had a whole slew of baby snakes. He called up the zoologist, and asked her how that was possible. She replied, "Well, you see, those snakes were adders. And everybody knows that to get adders to multiply you need log tables."

Old biologists never die, they just ferment away.

Life is a sexually transmitted disease.

Life is anything that dies when you stomp it!

Support bacteria - it's the only culture some people have!

A doctor, an engineer, and a fungal taxonomist arrived at The Pearly Gates.
The doctor said how he'd healed the sick, helped the lame; but he was a sinner and was sent to Hell.
The engineer told how he'd built homes for the homeless, etc.; but he messed up the environment, so he was sent to Hell.
The fungal taxonomist was frightened by all this, but as soon as he mentioned his occupation, God said "You've already been through Hell, Welcome to Heaven."

How do you tell the difference between boys and girls?
Take their genes down.

What are the four food groups?
For bachelors: Fast, Frozen, Junk and Spoiled.
For drinkers: Malt, Hops, Barley and Yeast.
For heavies: Caffeine, Fat, Sugar, Chocolate.

While driving down a steep and curvy logging road, a group of biologists loose control of their 4-wd "Jimmy" and careen down the hill. The truck piles up at the bottom of the canyon, and everyone aboard perishes. Surprisingly, they all go to heaven. At an orientation they are asked, "When you are in your casket and your friends and family are mourning about your death, what would you like to hear them say about you?"

The first guy, a well known botanist says, "I would like to hear them say that I was one of the greatest botanists of my time, and left an eternal contribution to the botanical world."

The second guy, an ornithologist, says, "I would like to hear that I was a wonderful birder and made a huge difference in the recovery of our bird populations."

The last guy, a scruffy mammalogist, replies, "I would like to hear them say... 'LOOK, HE'S MOVING!!!' "

A young college student had stayed up all night studying for his zoology test the next day. As he entered the classroom, he saw ten stands with ten birds on them with a sack over each bird and only the legs showing. He sat right on the front row because he wanted to do the best job possible. The professor announced that the test would be to look at each set of bird legs and give the common name, habitat, genus, species, etc. The student looked at each set of bird legs. They all looked the same to him. He began to get upset. He had stayed up all night studying, and now had to identify birds by their legs. The more he thought about it, the madder he got. Finally, he could stand it no longer. He went up to the professor's desk and said, "What a stupid test! How could anyone tell the difference between birds by looking at their legs?" With that the student threw his test on the professor's desk and walked out the door. The professor was surprised. The class was so big that he didn't know every student's name, so as the student reached the door the professor called, "Mister, what's your name?"

The enraged student pulled up his pant legs and said, "You guess, buddy! You guess!"

An old mountain man in Arkansas was sick and bedridden. He had not been outdoors for a few weeks and had a sharp craving for a meal of wild squirrel. He summoned his half-idiot son into the room and instructed him to go squirrel hunting and bring him back a squirrel or two. He also told his son to be very careful <u>not</u> to shoot the squirrel in the head as he would need its brains later to "tan" the squirrel's pelt. (Tanning a skin using the animal's brains is a common practice in certain areas, it generally takes about one brain to tan one skin).

The idiot son spent most of the day searching the woods for tree squirrels, but was not having any luck. Finally, high up in a sweet-gum tree, he spotted a squirrel's head sticking out from a hole. He remembered his Pa's admonitions to save the brains. After deciding he may not have another chance, he shot it in the head, thus ruining the brains.

His sick Pa was upset, "I can't tan that skin without no brains!" he said, "Now what am I a gonna do?" Thinking quickly, he remembered that up on the river there were 3 fisheries biologists doing some field work.

"Well, we're only tanning one squirrel skin, walk up the river and shoot one of them dang fish biologists and I'll use his brains to tan the skin," he told the son. The son did as he was told and soon returned with the prize. As it turned out, the brain wasn't large enough and the boy was upset as he would have to make another trip to harvest the other two biologist's brains.

"Look on the bright side, boy", the old man told him, "Two more ought to be just enough…. We'd have been in real trouble if they was botanists!"

Genetics explain why you look like your father and if you don't why you should.

Sterility is hereditary: If your grandfather didn't have children and your father didn't have children, you won't have children either.

What do you call a plant that is vericose and eats insects?
A venous fly trap.

What do you call the study of polyps?
Wart-iculture.

Who is the mother of the mother of a botanist?
A Granule.

What is the attitude of many botanists?
Haploid go luckoid.

Hastate makes wastate.

Why will shrubs rule the world?
They will have Hedge-mony.

What do you call a curly haired monoceous plant?
A perm-aphrodite.

What is a boring plant eater?
An Herbi-bore.

What do you call a plant eating pig?
An herbi-boar.

What do you say when a botanist sneezes?
HIRSUTE-ite.

How do horticulturists get across bodies of water?
With the help of a a Boat-anist.

Why was the botanist so wise?
He was very sage.

Which police show do agriculturists watch?
CROPS.

Do Botanists support stem cell research??

Do botanists have all the anthers??

The plant had his car stolon.

What was the greenhorn botanist sent on?
A stipe hunt.

How was the botanist paid?
With a stipe-nd.

What does a botanist call beurocratic red tape?
STIPULE-ations.

Who is a plants favorite action movie star?
Silvester Stolon.

What do botanists give electronically to show their love?
E-roses.

What do botanists wear on Mars?
A Spathe suit.

What does a successively layered animal need to breathe?
Exogen.

What is it called when you blackmail a flower?
Extrorsion.

Why are plant growths so upseting?
They have gall.

What is a service offered by the phone company to botanists?
Gall waiting.

How are seeds like bacteria?
They are both germs.

He so gibbous, and he so takeous.

How was the botanist able to recognize the nut?
At a glans.

Is a botanist a grafter??

Why are mosses so grouchy when they all lie on the same plane?
I guess they just like to Complanate.

How do botanists send mail?
Through the compost office.

Why did the plant eat meat?
It was coniferous.

How do relatives of weasels pollinate a plant?
They make it Ferretile.

The botanist was eaten by a cul-lion.

What do botanists run up to get excercise?
Hilum.

Which botanist is a Senator?
Senator Hilum Clinton.

Is a botanist from down South a Hilum Billy??

What part of a flower is in a car?
A Calyx converter.

What does a botanist studying jagged margins shoot from her bow?
Erose

Why are mosses so grouchy when they all lie on the same plane?
I guess they just like to Complanate.

How do botanists send mail?
Through the compost office.

Why did the plant eat meat?
It was coniferous.

How do relatives of weasels pollinate a plant?
They make it Ferretile.

The botanist was eaten by a cul-lion.

What do botanists run up to get excercise?
Hilum.

Is a botanist from down South a Hilum Billy??

What part of a flower is in a car?
A Calyx converter.

What does a botanist studying jagged margins shoot from her bow?
Erose.

How do leaf clusters start a duel?
They stand Bract to Bract.

What is the favorite beverage of a botanist?
Bud-wiser.

Which hooded flower married Marc Anthoney?
Calyptera patra.

After typing too much what did the botanist develop?
Carpel- tunnel syndrome.

What do you call an arch that is as wide as it is tall made out of soil?
A Cantena-ry.

How do botanists and soil scientists listen to satellites?
With Catenas.

How did the botanist, after dealing with fertilizer, clean her hands?
She had a manure-cure.

The happy botanist was looking very chipper.

Ah go fly a chitin.

Wacky definitions: bostryx
A city North of New yorkx.

What gaming system do botanists play on?
An Attar-ii.

What class did the tool for drilling holes have to take?
Auger management

Which growth promoting substance can also draw a plow?
Auxin.

Why are places capable of consuming cars?
They are Auto-trophic

Which sharp apendage will botanists play chess with?
A P-AWN.

What measure of a plants resilience also predicts their evolution?
The Hardy Wineburg equilibrium laws.

How do botanists catch bartenders?
With Barbates.

What is a marsh botanist's favoirte movie?
Bog to the Future.

Neither a lender nor a Bougher be.

What does an arborist eat soup in?
A Bole.

Why was the soil so good in school?
It knows its ABCs.

.Where was the plant leaf imprisoned?
In the pennate-enturary.

Who won in the plant politics race?
The Accumbent.

Who told the story of the plant soil's life?
The N-Aerator.

How does a Japanese botanist bid farewell?
Cyan-ara.

How to botanists tell computers what to do?
With apogamy language (a programing language).

The close fitting leaf was being appressed.

Where do monkey flowers live?
On the Ape-planate.

Which tree did the Japanese bomb on December 7 1942?
The Pearl Arbor.

Why was there no food around the tree?
Becasue the Arbor-eat-em.

I just bought a new book on plant care.
Why?
'Cause I want to be a good weeder!

How do you like that new gardening show?
I can take it or leaf it!

I really like that gardening show.
Yeah, it really grows on you!

Do you know how to ship vegetables?
By Parsley Post!

How do you tell a dogwood tree from a redwood tree?
I don't know! How?
Because of its bark!

Two friars are having trouble paying off the belfry, so they open a florist shop.
Everyone wants to buy flowers from the men of God so business is quickly booming.
The florist across town sees a huge drop in sales and asks the two friars to close their shop, but they refuse.
A month later the florist begs the friars to close because he's having trouble feeding his family.
Again, they refuse, so the florist hires Hugh McTaggert.
Hugh is the roughest, toughest thug in town and is hired to "persuade" the friars to close.
Hugh asks the friars to close their florist shop.
When they refuse, he threatens to beat the crap out of them and wreck their shop every day they remain open, so they close.

This proves once again that Hugh and only Hugh can prevent florist friars

New gardeners learn by trowel and error.

If I could only grow green stuff in my garden like I can in my refrigerator.

Two older ladies were sitting on a park bench outside the local town hall where a flower show was in progress.

One leaned over and said, "Life is so boring. We never have any fun anymore. For $5.00 I'd take my clothes off right now and streak through that stupid flower show!"
"You're on!" said the other old lady, holding up a $5.00 bill.
As fast as she could, the first little old lady fumbled her way out of her clothes and, completely naked, streaked through the front door of the flower show.
Waiting outside, her friend soon heard a huge commotion inside the hall, followed by loud applause. The naked lady burst out through the door surrounded by a cheering crowd.
"What happened?" asked her waiting friend.
"Why, I won first prize for Best Dried Arrangement."

Knowledge is knowing a tomato is a fruit;
Wisdom is not putting it in a fruit salad

What is a plant's favorite number?
Tree!

Where was the plant leaf imprisoned?
In the pennate-enturary

Who won in the plant politics race?
The Accumbent

Who told the story of the plant soil's life?
The N-Aerator

How does a Japanese botanist bid farewell?
Cyan-ara

What measure of a plants resilience also predicts their evolution?
The Hardy Wineburg equilibrium laws

How do botanists catch bartenders?
With Barbates

What is a marsh botanist's favorite movie?
Bog to the Future

Neither a lender nor a Bougher be.

After typing too much what did the botanist develop?
Carpel- tunnel syndrome.

How did the botanist, after dealing with fertilizer, clean her hands?
She had a manure-cure

The happy botanist was looking very chipper.

Is a botanist from down South a Hilum Billy?

Is a botanist a grafter?

Why is bach's concerto like a plant?
Both are organic

What does a botanists do when he/she finds a new orchid?
Labellum

Students in an AP Biology class were taking their mid-term exam. The last question was: "Name seven advantages of 'Mother's Milk'.... The students had to answer all seven advantages, or he/she would get no credit. One thoughtful young man turned in the following exam

1. It is perfect formula for the child.

2. It provides immunity against several diseases.

3. It is always at the right temperature.

4. It is inexpensive.

5. It bonds the child to mother, and vice versa.

6. It is always available as needed.

He got stuck and couldn't think of another advantage. He had completed the rest of the exam. He knew how important seven points were toward the final score. Finally, in desperation, as the bell rang, and as tests were being collected, he wrote: The containers are so cute.

A boy was assigned a paper on childbirth and asked his mother, "How was I born?"
"Well honey..." said the slightly prudish mother, "the stork brought you to us."
"Oh," said the boy, "and how did you and daddy get born?"
"Oh, the stork brought us too."
"Well how were grandpa and grandma born?" the boy persisted.
"Well darling, the stork brought them too!" said the mother, by now starting to squirm a little.
Several days later, the boy handed in his paper to the teacher who read with confusion the opening sentence: "This report has been very difficult to write due to the fact that there

hasn't been a natural childbirth in my family for three generations."

A wildlife biologist had been in Africa for many years, studying elephant behavior. On one trip out into the jungle he had observed an adult elephant limping behind the pack. He watched the elephant with his scope and could see a terrible sore on the elephant's foot with a huge thorn sticking from the oozing hole. The elephant seemed in such pain that the biologist decided to risk his life and remove the thorn. He mustered his courage and walked up to the beast. Slowly he reached down and grabbed the end of the thorn. With a big yank, he pulled the thorn from the animal's wound. The elephant screamed and spun to face the biologist. He stood there paralyzed with fear as the animal stared him in the eyes. After a moment, the elephant reached out to gently pat him with it's truck and then disappeared into the jungle. This touching moment had stayed with the biologist for many years. One day he was visiting a local zoo with his son when a huge elephant rushed through it's exhibit and stopped at the edge of the fence. The animal stared at the biologist and longingly reached it's truck toward him. As the elephant stared at him, he recalled the tender moment shared with an elephant many years before. "Could this be that very same elephant?....It must be!" he thought. After having the animal stare at him for some time, he was overcome with a tender familiarity and climbed over the fence to get closer to the gentle beast. When he reached the animal, it reached out it's truck and picked the biologist off the ground by his legs. After slamming his body on the ground a few times, it bashed him against a tree and threw his body over the fence and back into the crowd of visitors. I guess it wasn't the same elephant.

Ben was assigned a new wildlife technician and she was driving him crazy. She was blonde and pretty and insisted on carrying beauty products in a little field bag - nail polish, hair care products, gels, creams and so on.

One day they were driving the rugged four-wheel drive down a dirt road when a big rabbit ran in front of them and was hit by the truck. Ben pulls over and walks back to the dead rabbit. He felt terrible, but there was clearly nothing he could do for the dead creature.

His blonde partner pipes in and yells, "Wait, I have just the thing!"

She races back to the truck and begins to rifle through her beauty products. Ben watches as brushes and combs fly from the bag. Finally she races back with an aerosol can and sprays the dead rabbit with it's contents. Immediately the rabbit springs to its feet, waves goodbye, hops a few feet, pauses and waves again. The rabbit repeats this strange behavior...wave-hop-wave-hop, until it disappears over the hill.

Ben is amazed and asks, "What in the world is in that can?"

The blonde biologists says, " Duh...look at the label."

 "Hair Spray .... Immediately revives dead hair and creates a permanent wave"

A logger is driving down the highway and sees two botanists trying to measure the height of a small pine tree. Their tape measure is not long enough so one botanist stands on the shoulders of the other and attempts to extend the tape to the tree top but it is not long enough. While trying, he falls to the ground. They attempt this about five times and each time the top botanist falls. The logger is laughing but feels sorry for the pair, gets out of his truck, takes out an electric saw and cuts down the tree. The botanists are looking at him like he is crazy. He then takes a tape measure and measures the tree. "OK guys, the tree is 14' 6." He then gets in his truck and drives away. The two botanists are stunned and speechless. Finally one says to the other ,"How do you like that, we are trying to measure the height of the tree and that stupid jerk measures the width."

An atheist biologist was walking through the woods one day.

"What majestic trees"! "What powerful rivers"! "What beautiful animals"! He said to himself.

As he was walking alongside the river, he heard a rustling in the bushes behind him. He turned to look. He saw a 7-foot grizzly charge towards him. He ran as fast as he could up the path. He looked over his shoulder & saw that the bear was closing in on him. He looked over his shoulder again, & the bear was even closer. He tripped & fell on the ground. He rolled over to pick himself up but saw that the bear was right on top of him, reaching for him with his left paw & raising his right paw to strike him. At that instant the Atheist cried out, "Oh my God!" Time Stopped. The bear froze. The forest was silent.

As a bright light shone upon the man, a voice came out of the sky. "You deny my existence for all these years, teach others I don't exist and even credit my beautiful creation to a cosmic accident". "Do you expect me to help you out of this predicament? Am I to count you as a believer"? The atheist looked directly into the light, "It would be hypocritical of me to suddenly ask You to treat me as a Christian now, but perhaps You could make the BEAR a Christian"?

"Very Well," said the voice. The light went out. The sounds of the forest resumed. And the bear dropped his right paw, brought both paws together, bowed his head & spoke: "Lord bless this food, which I am about to eat, Amen."

A wildlife biology grad student was writing a proposal to get some funding for a mongoose research project. He sat at his computer and typed:

"I will attach radio collars to a pair of mongooses...."

Wait, he thought, that doesn't sound right. So, he backspaced and began again:

"I will attach radio collars to a pair of mongeese...."

Still again, he thought, that just doesn't sound right. He backspaced again, and after thinking for several minutes, he began to type:

"I will attach a radio collar to an adult mongoose.

Immediately after the first is attached, I will, attach a second collar to another mongoose..."

An 8th grade boy was doing some research for his career report at school. He asks his dad, "Father, how many wildlife biologists work for the Federal Government?"
"The honest father replies, "Oh, I would say at least half of 'em."

A University had advertised for two biologists to help in their mammalogy department, specifically with a group of captive grizzly bears. They had only two applicants - a beautiful young women biologist and an older male biologist.
The mammalogist in charge of the project knew that not everyone can handle working with such fierce creatures so he decided to test their skills with the bears. The two hopefuls followed him out to the bear pen. He first asked the young women to show him what she could do.
She entered the cage, stripped down to her bikini, and the largest bear walked up and nuzzled her bare legs.
The astonished mammalogist then said to the old man, "Can you do that?"
"You're darn right I can," said the old man, "just get that bear out of there first !"

A wildlife biologist is working in the woods, miles from the nearest town. He's camped alone with his dog and cat as his companions. Suddenly, an old gentleman carrying a small limp dog, franticly runs into his camp.
"Please, please help me! I think something has happened to Willie. Our Winnebago is parked just around the bend and we've seen you camped here. We didn't know what to do. We thought of you because we had seen all this scientific equipment laying around here. Can you help him?"
" Sir, I'm not a vet, I'm a wildlife biologist," the young biologist told the worried man.
"Can you please just have a look at him, I'll pay you anything you need. I just need to know. If he's still alive, maybe I can

rush him into town."

"Ok, put him here on the table." The young biologist looks the limp dog over, but its plain that the dog is dead,, no pulse or signs of breathing.

"I'm sorry sir, but I'm afraid poor Willie is dead."
"No, I can't believe that..... It can't be true...are you sure?"
"Yes, I'm quite sure."
"I just can't believe that....With all this equipment, isn't there something you can do? I must be absolutely sure."
The biologist called his big yellow cat over to the table. The cat walked around the dead dog, occasionally sniffing at the carcass. He then looks up at the biologist and let out a few weak meows.
"Well, the cat say he's dead. Does that assure you?"
"No, I need more than that...Do you have anything else?"
The biologist calls over his big black dog. The dog circles the body a few times, sniffing it every now and then. After a few moments, the dog barks at the biologist.
"Well, now the dog says he's dead. That's all I can do for you sir."
"OK, well I guess its true. I'll take him back and bury him...How much do I owe you?"
"It'll be $650 bucks." The biologist tells the old man.
"What??", replied the old man, "How can you charge that much?"
"Well sir, I could have told you he was dead for only a dollar, but you're the one that insisted on the cat scan and the lab tests!"

According to the Knight-Ridder News Service, the inscription on the metal bands used by the U.S. Department of the Interior to tag migratory birds has been changed. The bands used to bear the address of the Washington Biological Survey, abbreviated -- Wash. Biol. Surv. -- until the agency received the following letter from an Arkansas camper:

"Dear Sirs:
While camping last week I shot one of your birds. I think it was a crow. I followed the cooking instructions on the leg tag and I want to tell you it was horrible."
The bands are now marked Fish and Wildlife Service.

Biology Pick Up Lines:

The only cleavage I want to see is at a cellular level.

If we were like chromosomes, you'd be my homologous pair .
Baby, I wish I were DNA Helicase, so I could unzip your genes.

Girl whenever I'm near you, I undergo anaerobic respiration because you take my breath away.

If I was an endoplasmic reticulum, how would you want me: Smooth or Rough?

I wish I was adenine, then I could get paired with U.

Your chromosomes have combined beautifully.

Girl, your so hot you denature my proteins.

I like my sex the way I like my endoplasmic reticulum.....Rough.

You must be a gibberelin, because I'm experiencing some stem elongation.

Baby, every time I see you, my cardiovascular system gets all worked up

Chemistry Jokes

"All that glitters is not gold, but at least it contains free electrons"

(Fe)male...male with iron added, for greater strength, ductility, and magnetism.

C Ho Co La Te
"Better living through Chemistry"

What did the mass spectrophotometer say to the gas chromoatograph?
Breaking up is hard to do.

Organic chemistry is the chemistry of carbon compounds.
Biochemistry is the study of carbon compounds that crawl.

What emotional disorder does a gas chomatograph suffer from?
Separation anxiety.

What kind of dog does a chemist scientist have? A Laboratory Retriever!

Chemicals: Noxious substances from which modern foods are made.

Have you heard the one about a chemist who was reading a book about helium and just couldn't put it down?

If you're not part of the solution, you're part of the precipitate!

If two bears, one in Yosemite and one in Alaska, fall into the water. which one dissolves faster?
The one in Alaska because it is Polar.

How many physical chemists does it take to wash a beaker?
None. That's what organic chemists are for!

Oxidants happen.

Do I know any good chemistry jokes?
Sorry, I can't zinc of any.

Some oxygen molecules help fires burn while others help make water, so sometimes it's brother against brother.

To most people solutions mean finding the answers. But to chemists solutions are things that are still all mixed up.

In looking at a drop of water under a microscope, we find there are twice as many H's as O's.

How many physical chemists does it take to change a light bulb?
 Only one, but he'll change it three times, plot a straight line through the data, and then extrapolate to zero concentration.

Little Johnny's teacher asks, "What is the chemical formula for water?"
Little Johnny replies, "HIJKLMNO!"
The teacher, puzzled, asks, "What on Earth are you talking about?"
Johnny replies, "Yesterday you said it was H to O!"

A small piece of sodium which lived in a test tube fell in love with a Bunsen burner.
"Oh Bunsen, my flame. I melt whenever I see you . . .", the sodium pined.
"It's just a phase you're going through", replied the Bunsen burner.

What is the dieter's element?
Nobelium

A teacher was lecturing on the conditions in which bacteria exist. Elaborating on the acidic environment where bacteria thrive, he suggested a simple experiment. "I want you to drop a nail into a glass of Coke or Pepsi, and then observe the acidic reaction on the nail," he said.
 The girl sitting in the back raised her hand and asked in all seriousness, "Do you mean a real nail, or a press-on?"

Two students who wanted to celebrate the long and light summer evening by fishing in their boat. But first they went to the lab, grabbed a bottle with the magic label 96%, and set off. After some time, the one said to the other, "I am afraid we have done something wrong. This is not ethanol, it is sulphuric acid."
"I know. I have just peed a hole in the boat."

If H_2O is water, what is H_2O_4?
H_2O_2 is for drinking, bathing, cleaning…

Organic chemistry causes alkynes of trouble.

Experience is directly proportional to equipment ruined.

Scarecrows make the best chemists.
They're out standing in their fields.

No, a covalent bond isn't an illicit relationship between two nuns.

No, mixed bed resins isn't a farce by Moliere.

How many physical chemists does it take to change a light bulb?
Only one, but he'll change it three times, plot a straight line through the data, and then extrapolate to zero concentration.

What weapon can you make from the Chemicals Potassium, Nickel and Iron?
KNiFe.

Two chemists meet for the first time at a symposium. One is American, one is British. The British chemists asks the American chemist, "So what do you do for research?"
The American responds, "Oh, I work with arsoles."
The Brit responds, "Yes, sometimes my colleagues piss me off also."

Where do you extract Mercury from?
Hg Wells.

How did the chemist survive the famine?

How do chemists avoid starvation?
By subsisting on titrations.

A female student wished to make some potassium hydroxide solution (aqueous) and decided to throw a large lump of potassium into a bucket of water. Her professor observed what she was about to do, out of the corner of his eye and hurried towards her, and after confirming this was what she was intending to do, asked her first to stir the water in the bucket for five minutes before adding the potassium. She was puzzled and ran after him to ask the purpose of this action.
"It will give me time to get away" said the professor.

What element do women use to get dates?
Tellurium.

What is a chemist's favorite house plant?
Germanium.

How did the chemist die?
Oxidentally.

Sodium, sodium, sodium, sodium, sodium, sodium, sodium, sodium: Batman.

The chemistry professor was demonstrating the properties ofvarious acids. "Now I'm going to drop this silver coin into this glass of acid. Will it dissolve?"
"No sir," one student called out.
"No?" queried the professor. "Perhaps you can explain why the silver won't dissolve in this particular acid."
"Because if it would, you wouldn't have dropped it in!"

A super-saturated solution is one that holds more than it can hold.

Never make chemists angry?
They overreact.

What does a chemist do that can't swim?
Zinc.

A couple of months in the laboratory can frequently save a couple of hours in the library.

Why did the chicken cross the road?
The chicken crossed the road because there were too many moles of chicken on the reactants side of the road equilibrium.

What kind of car do chemists drive?
Mercedes Benzenes.

Why do chemists like "Talk Like A Pirate" day?
They can say "ARRRRRGHon"

Love is chemistry.
Sex is physics.

What did the cowboy do with his horse?

Rhodium.

Teacher: Johnny, what's H_2SO_4?
Johnny : Er, hang on. I know this one. It's on the tip of my tongue...
Teacher: Well spit it out quick! It's sulfuric acid!

What did the gambler do with his cards?
Palladium.

Relationships are like titrations.
Just take it slow and don't over react.

What's a cation afraid of?
A dogion.

Who leaves the chemist brightly colored eggs every year?
The Ether Bunny

Do you know the Spanish word for silicon?
Si.

Wanna hear a joke about element 116?
UUH...

What's the formula for water?
H-two-O.

What's the formula for an ice cube?
H-two-O-CUBED.

Following sodium fusion the professor asked a struggling co-ed student
"Have you found anything yet?"
"Erm... er...I...er... Its nearly Chlorine!"
Professor, "Don't be silly. It can't be NEARLY chlorine, that's like deing nearly pregnant. You can't be nearly pregnant!"
Co-ed: "You don't get around much, do you!"

What do you get when you combine a liberal arts major with O2?
An oxymoron

It takes alkynes to make a world. Chemical engineers do it in packed beds.

Chemists do it in test tubes.

Chemists do it in the fume hood.

Chemists do it periodically on table.

Chemists do it reactively.

Chemists like to experiment.

Polymer chemists do it in chains.

Electrochemists have greater potential.

Organic chemists do it on the bench. But seriously, its pHun!

How do you make ethyl fornicate?
With ethanol!

Free radicals have revolutionized chemistry.

Why do chemists like nitrates so much?
They're cheaper than day rates.

Old chemists never die, they just fail to react.

Old chemists never die they just reach equilibrium

Old chemists never die, they just smell that way.

Old chemists never die, they just do it inorganically.

Old chemists never die, they just lose their refluxes.

What do chemists use to make guacomole?
Avogadros.

What do you get if you chop an Avogadro up into 6.02 X 10^23 pieces?
Guaca-MOLE!

What did the Italian chemist say when he became becalmed whilst sailing?
Avagadro (I've a gotta row).

Did you hear about the chemist that fell into the esterification vat?
They managed to save his life but he was left terribly butylated.

One day he was approached by his assistant who all excited informed him that he had just discovered a universal solvent.
Liebig asked: "And what is a universal solvent?"
Assistant: "One that dissolves all substances."
Liebig: "Where are you going to keep that solvent, then?"

When a chemist says "Put it in a round bottom" it doesn't mean what you think it means.

I'm positive that a free electron once stripped me of an electron after he lepton me. You gotta keep your ion them.

Water is composed of two gins, oxygin and hydrogin.
Oxygin is pure gin. Hydrogin is gin and water.

A chemistry teacher was berating the students for not learning the Periodic Table of the Elements. She said, 'Why when I was your age I knew both their names and weights.'

One pupil opined, 'Yeah, but Miss, there were so few of them back then.'

Titanium is the nymphomaniac metal. When it gets hot, it combines with
anything.

Ban Dihydrogen Monoxide!
1. It can cause excessive sweating and vomiting
2. It is a major component in acid rain
3. It can cause severe burns in its gaseous state
4. Accidental inhalation can kill you
5. It contributes to erosion
6. It decreases effectiveness of automobile brakes
7. It has been found in tumors of terminal cancer patients

Chemists do like to mix it up.

How many atoms in a guacamole?
Avocado's number.

How do you make a 24 molar solution?
Put you artificial teeth in water.

What kind of ghosts haunt chemistry faculties?
Methylated Spirits.

Did you hear about the industrialist who had a huge chloroform spill at his
factory?
His business went insolvent.

How do you get lean molecules?
Feed them titrations.

Why are chemists perfect for solving problems?
Because they have all the solutions.

Chemical: A substance that:
1) An organic chemist turns into a foul odor;
2) An analytical chemist turns into a procedure;
3) A physical chemist turns into a straight line;
4) A biochemist turns into a helix;
5) A chemical engineer turns into a profit.

How can you tell a chemist from an AFL-CIO member?
By the way they pronounce "unionized."

Why did the chemicals refuse to react?
They were unionized.

Never throw sodim hloride at people.
That's a salt.

Chemical Engineering: The practice of doing for a profit what
an organic
chemist only does for fun.

Why does hamburger have lower energy than steak?
Because it's in the ground state.

What do you call a swim team made up of girls named
Jennifer?
Hydrogens.

Evaporation Allowance: The volume of alcohol that the
graduate students
can drink in a year's time.

Did you hear about the chemist who fell into the
methoxybenzene reactor and made anisole of himself?

Monomer: One mer.
Polymer: Many mers.

Which acid can spend his entire life in devotion?
Acetic acid.

If all the acids has to participate to the Olympic games, which one would win all the gold?
Performic acid.

Physical Chemistry: The pitiful attempt to apply y=mx+b to everything in the universe.

I love you for who you are.
A chemistry major that knows how to make LSD.

Three wise chemists walk into a Bethlehem stable. Seeing the son of god lying in his manger, they tell Mary they have brought three gifts. They drop to their knees and each give the baby Jesus an isomer of [Au(NO2)(CO)2].
Gold, FAC n' CIS and MER.

When asked if she wanted a PB and J sandwich for lunch, Jane said no I don't want a Lead and Jelly sandwich!

Argon: Someone stole the letter between Q and S!

I'm just one accident away from being a super villain.

Research: That which I do for the benefit of humanity, you do for the money, he does to hog all the glory.

Kekule, who conceptualized the Benzene Ring was sitting at the bar at the Scientists Ball expounding on how the whole idea had come to him in a dream.
"That's very interesting." said the man sitting next to him.
"Oh yeah! And who might you be?" he asked.
"I'm Robert Chesebrough." said the man.
"And what are you famous for might I ask?"
"Not much ... but I did invent petroleum jelly ... you know Vaseline!"
"And how did you dream up that idea?"
"Oh, I didn't dream it at all ... I got it from my pet parrot ... the one with a speech impediment."
"Oh really ... now just how did that happen?"

"Well I was working with crude oils back when Rockefeller was making his fortune in the industry and we had all these by-products that were being dumped into a stream and I was thinking about how they could be put to good use. I was out for a walk in the park one day with my pet parrot on my shoulder when she spied a rather large duck! She immediately squawked "Poly wants a Quacker". I realized that it would put her to great stress so I came up with Vaseline."

Chemistry puts the "cation" in education.

I was studying chemistry in college but by third year I was out of my element.

Toxicology: The wholesale slaughter of white rats bred especially for that purpose.

What is acetone's favorite big-screen actor?
Michael Ketone.

Propane: My dentist doesn't believe in anesthesia. He's propane.

Heard about the man who poisoned his wife with a razor?
He gave her arse a nick.

What do you call too many cows on one side of a ship?
A catalyst!

What is a chemist's favorite fast food?
Bunsen Burgers.

When you don't know what you're doing, do it neatly.

The road to hell is paved with sloppy analysis.

Hydrogen and Oxygen are in a bar having a drink when Gold walks in and both say:

Au get outta the bar

What is a mortician's favorite element? Barium & Krypton

What are a doctor's favorite elements? Helium & Curium

What is a robber's least favorite element? Copper

What is a stage performers favorite element? Actinium

What is Pat Sajak's favorite element? Vanadium

What is Mickey Mouse's favorite element? Plutonium

What is a geneticist's favorite element? Mendelevium

What is Saddam Hussein's favorite element? Cesium

What is a nymphomaniac's favorite element? Fermium

What is George Bush's favorite element? Protactinium

What is a friend's favorite element? Palladium

What is Monty Python's favorite element? Nickel

What is Dr. Watson's favorite element? Holmium

What is a tourist's favorite element? Europium, Germanium, Francium

What is the Cowardly Lion's favorite element? Osmium

What is a tailor's favorite element? Sodium

What is an hit man's favorite element? Iridium

What is a guy's favorite element? Gallium

What is a captain's least favorite element? Zinc

What is a programmer's favorite element? Carbon

What is a plowman's favorite element? Oxygen

What is a baker's favorite element? Flourine

What is an orthopedic surgeon's favorite element? Neon

What is Odysseus' favorite element? Beryllium

What is a draftsman's favorite element? Cadmium

What is Margaret's defense against rape? Magnesium

What is Mrs. Pacino's favorite element? Aluminum

What is a prison's funniest element? Silicon

What is "Happy Days" favorite element? Phosphorus

What element inspired famous designer jeans? Calcium

What is a steam rollers favorite element? Platinum

What is a fax machine's favorite element? Scandium

What is Prince Charles' favorite element? Polonium

What is a Usenet Users favorite element? Radon

What is a morning person's favorite element? Americium

What is a Hayes Modem's favorite element? Astatine

What is San Francisco's favorite element? Titanium

What is Frisco's second favorite element? Uranium

What is Frisco's third favorite element? Bismuth

What is Odin's favorite element? Chromium

What is a college registrar's favorite element? Iron

What is used car dealers favorite element? Selenium

What is Mad Max's favorite element? Rhodium

What is a music lover's favorite element? Cadmium

What is the clergyman's least favorite element? Tin

What is the KGB's least favorite element? Tellurium

What is the football player's least favorite element? Hafnium

What is a thespian's favorite element? Actinium

What is a bald man's favorite element? Chromium

What is a C programmer's favorite element? Argon

What is a three year old's favorite element? Yttrium

What is the friendliest element? Hydrogen

What element is not as friendly? Gold

What element is always leaving? Copper

What is the least truthful element Lithium

Which element is least liked at a party? Boron

What element do you use to clean a thunderbucket?
Potassium

Where do you get Jovian fast food? Iodine-r

Rules Of The Lab

1. When you don't know what you're doing, do it neatly.

2. Experiments must be reproducible, they should fail the same way each
time.

3. First draw your curves, then plot your data.

4. Experience is directly proportional to equipment ruined.

5. A record of data is essential, it shows you were working.

6. To study a subject best, understand it thoroughly before you start.

7. To do a lab really well, have your report done well in advance.

8. If you can't get the answer in the usual manner, start at the answer and
derive the question.

9. If that doesn't work, start at both ends and try to find a common middle.

10. In case of doubt, make it sound convincing.

11. Do not believe in miracles--rely on them.

12. Team work is essential. It allows you to blame someone else.

13. All unmarked beakers contain fast-acting, extremely toxic poisons.

14. Any delicate and expensive piece of glassware will break before any use can be made of it. (Law of Spontaneous Fission)

Engineering Jokes

What is the definition of an engineer? Answer: Someone who solves a problem you didn't know you had, in a way you don't understand.

Question: What is the difference between engineer boots and cowboy boots?
Answer: Cowboy boots have the bull-crap on the outside!

One day a group of engineers got together and decided that man had come a long way and no longer needed God. They picked one engineer to go and tell Him that they were done with Him.
The engineer walked up to God and said, "God, we've decided that we no longer need you. We're to the point that we can clone people and do many miraculous things, so why don't you just go on and get lost."God listened patiently to the man and after the engineer was done talking, God said, "Very well! How about this? Let's have a man-making contest."
The man replied, "Okay, great!"
But God added, "Now we're going to do this just like I did back in the old days with Adam." The engineers said, "Sure, no problem." He bent down and grabbed himself a handful of dirt.
God just looked at him and said, "No, no, no. Go get your own dirt!"

The instructor was demonstrating the wonders of static electricity to his
class at MIT. While holding a plastic rod in one hand and a wool cloth inthe other, he told the class, "You can see that I get a large charge from rubbing my rod..."
That was pretty much the end of learning for that day.

If you dropped a cat with a piece of buttered toast tied to its back this is the secret of levitation. Toast ALWAYS lands butter side down, but cats always land on their feet, so the combination will hover just above ground level rotating, neither the cat nor toast able to land.

An engineer is a fellow that takes a measurement with a micrometer, marks it with a crayon, and cuts it with an axe.

Nitrogen is not found in Ireland because it is not found in a free state.

3 engineers and 3 accountants were taking a trip to a conference. At the train station, each accountant bought their ticket. However, the engineers only bought one ticket for all three of them. The accountants asked how they were going to get away with only having one ticket, and the engineers told them to watch and see.
After they boarded the train and it started moving, all three engineers locked themselves in the bathroom. When the conductor came to collect the tickets, he knocked on the door. The door cracked open and a hand shot out with the ticket. The conductor, not knowing that there were three people inside, took it and moved on. After he left the car the engineers came out. The accountants, were impressed, and told the engineers that they would try the same trick on the return trip.
On the way back, the accountants got one ticket, but the engineers didnt get any. The accountants laughed and wondered how the engineers were going to get themselves out of this one. After everyone boarded the train, and it started moving, the engineers hid in one bathroom, while the accountants did the same in the other one. Just before the conductor entered the car, one of the engineers came out, walked up to the accountants' bathroom, and knocked on the door.

Question: What do engineers use for birth control?
Answer: Their personality.

Some people say the glass is half full, others say it's half empty. Engineers say the glass is twice as large as it needs to be.

One day in heaven, the Lord decided He would visit the earth and take a stroll. Walking down the road, He encountered a man who was crying.
The Lord asked the man, "Why are you crying, my son?" The man said that he was blind and had never seen a sunset. The Lord touched the man who could then see and was happy.
As the Lord walked further, He met another man crying and asked, "Why are you crying, my son?" The man was born a cripple and was never able to walk. The Lord touched him and he could walk and he was happy.
Farther down the road, the Lord met another man who was crying and asked, "Why are you crying, my son?" The man said, "Lord, I am an engineer."
...and the Lord sat down and cried with him.

There once was a young engineer, who having worked for several years, decided that hc and his family should have a weekend getaway place. He searched the surrounding country, and found a lovely spot with frontage on a small river. They built a cabin, and began spending time there every chance they got. The kids loved it, and friends came for the quiet and fishing.
The engineer, however, wanted something unique for his cabin. He had been an award-winning pole vaulter in college. He therefore built a set of poles with a crosspiece, and a mulched run. He bought a new carbon fiber vaulting pole, new shoes, and was set. He would set off down the run, plant his pole, soar over the crosspiece, and land in the river with a satisfying splash. What a great way to spend a hot afternoon. He tried to teach a few friends to vault, with no success.
He enjoyed his cabin for years, and went out early in the

spring one year. It had been a very wet winter, lots of rain afterward. When the family arrived, the river was up and flowing at a good clip, with twice the usual current flowing. The engineer was determined to enjoy a few vaults into the water, but his wife didn't think it was safe. But, he was a good swimmer, and proceeded to have a go at it. His run and jump were flawless, he hit the water in good form, but upon surfacing, he was swept downstream and disappeared. His body was found later that day, tangled in streamside debris. It was a sad end for the engineer, and the family sold the cabin, with no desire to return to the scene of such tragedy. Our lamented engineer was a Civil Engineer. Had he consulted one of his Electrical Engineer brethren, he would have been warned that "It's not vaultage that kills you, it's the current!"

A mathematician, a physicist, and an engineer were all given a red rubber ball and told to find the volume. The mathematician carefully measured the diameter and evaluated a triple integral. The physicist filled a beaker with water, put the ball in the water, and measured the total displacement. The engineer looked up the model and serial numbers in his red-rubber-ball table.

Three condemned people are to be executed via the guillotine. First condemned person steps up, a minister. Switch is pulled. Blade doesn't come down. Minister cries out: "God knows I am innocent!" He's pardoned. Second condemned person is a revolutionary agitator. Switch is pulled. Blade doesn't come down. Guy cries out: "The revolution cannot be stopped!" He's pardoned.
Third condemned is an engineer. Same deal. He looks up, points up, says, "I think your problem is that the cable is binding right here..."

How do you tell an extrovert engineer from an introvert? And extrovert engineer will look at your shoes when he talks to you.

Around the start of the 20th century., A very famous electrical engineer gave up his trade and decided to travel around the world and discover other cultures. On his way back through the US, he stumbled upon a very poor and isolated Navajo village. He was so awed that his fellow Americans could be living in such destitution, that he sought out the Chief, to see what he could do to help. After several hours, the engineer finally succeeded in explaining the concept of electricity to the Chief, he implored the Chief to think of some way to implement the new technology.

After a few minutes, the Chief scratched his head and said, "Well, you know the outhouse is very cold and dark in the winter. Perhaps a light bulb would make that a better place for our people.

Needless to say, the engineer fulfilled the request, and became the first tourist to wire ahead for a reservation.

Five surgeons were taking a coffee break and were discussing their work. The first said, "I think accountants are the easiest to operate on. You open them up and everything inside is numbered."

The second said, "I think librarians are the easiest to operate on. You open them up and everything inside is in alphabetical order."

The Third said, "I like to operate on electricians. You open them up and everything inside is color-coded."

The fourth one said, "I like to operate on lawyers. They're heartless, spineless, gutless, and their heads and their butts are interchangeable."

Fifth surgeon said, "I like Engineers...they always understand when you have a few parts left over at the end..."

Engineers do not believe in luck nearly as much as they rely on it.

A mathematician, a biologist and a physicist are sitting in a street cafe watching people going in and coming out of the house on the other side of the street. First they see two

people going into the house. Time passes. After a while they notice three persons coming out of the house. The physicist: "The measurement wasn't accurate.".
The biologist: "They have reproduced".
The mathematician: "If now exactly one person enters the house then it will be empty again."

A engineer gets home from work and sees a note on the fridge from his wife. "This isn't working, I'm at my moms". he opens the fridge and checks the light, then grabs a beer and feels it cold. The engineer thinks to himself. "The fridge works fine"

It seems the U.S. Federal Aviation Administration has a unique device for testing the strength of windshields on airplanes.
The device is a gun that launches dead chicken at a plane's windshield at approximately the speed the plane flies.
The theory is that if the windshield doesn't crack from the carcass impact, it'll survive a real collision with a bird during flight.
It seems the British were very interested in this and wanted to test a windshield on a brand new, speedy locomotive they're developing.
They borrowed the FAA's chicken launcher, loaded the chicken and fired. The ballistic chicken shattered the windshield, went through the engineer's chair, broke an instrument panel and embedded itself in the back wall of the engine cab. The British were stunned and asked the FAA to recheck the test to see if everything was done correctly.
The FAA reviewed the test thoroughly and had one recommendation:
"Use a thawed chicken."

Three men: a project manager, a software engineer, and a hardware engineer are in Ft. Lauderdale for a two-week period helping out on a project.
About mid-week, they decide to walk up and down the beach

during their lunch hour. Halfway up the beach, they stumbled upon a lamp. They rubbed the lamp, and a genie appeared and said, "Normally, I would grant you three wishes, but since there are 3 of you, I will grant you each one wish."

The hardware engineer went first. "I would like to spend the rest of my life living in a huge house in St. Thomas, with no money worries and surrounded by beautiful women who worship me." The genie granted him his wish and sent him off to St. Thomas."

The software engineer went next. "I would like to spend the rest of my life living on a huge yacht cruising the Mediterranean, with no money worries and surrounded by beautiful women who worship me."

The genie sent him off to the Mediterranean.

Last, but not least it was the project manager's turn. "And what would your wish be?" asked the genie.

"I want them both back after lunch," replied the project manager.

What is the difference between a chemist and a chemical engineer?
 Oh, about $10 K a year.

Repeal Ohm's Law!

What do electrical engineers have for breakfast?
Ohmlets.

How to electrical engineers meditate?
Ohmmmmm.

An ounce of application is worth a pound of abstraction.

How do you recognize a field service engineer on the side of the road with a flat tire?
He's changing each tire to see which one is flat.

And the related problem:

How do you recognize a field service engineer on the side of the road who has run out of gas? ...
He's changing each tire to see which one is flat.

In the high school gym, all the girls were lined up against one wall, and all the boys against the opposite wall. Then, every 10 seconds, they walked toward each other until they were half the previous distance apart. A mathematician, a physicist, and an engineer were asked, "When will the girls and boys meet?"
The mathematician answered, "Never."
The physicist answered, "In an infinite amount of time."
The engineer answered, "Well, in about two minutes, they'll be close enough for all practical purposes."

Reaching the end of a job interview, the Human Resources person asked the young engineer fresh out of MIT, "And what starting salary were you looking for?"
The engineer said, "In the neighborhood of $100,000 a year, depending on the benefit's package."
The HR Person said, "Well, what would you say to a package of 5-weeks vacation, 14 paid holidays, full medical and dental, company matching retirement fund to 50% of salary, and a company car leased every 2 years - say, a red Corvette?"
The engineer sat up straight and said, "Wow!!! Are you kidding?"
And the HR Person said, "Of course, ...but you started it."

Engineers aren't boring people, we just get excited over boring things.

A physicist, a mathematician, and an engineer are staying in a hotel. Outside their rooms, a fire erupts.
The physicist steps outside to see the fire along with a bucket and water spigot. He simply fills the bucket with water and pours it on the flames until they go out then returns to bed.

The engineer steps outside to see the fire along with the bucket and water spigot. He meticulously calculates the amount of water needed and the rate of flow to most efficiently and effectively put out the fire. After a few minutes and a couple tests, the fire is extinguished.

The mathematician steps outside and sees the fire. He also notices the bucket and water spigot and exclaims "Their exists a solution" and returns to bed.

There is a half glass of scotch on a table.

The Arts student says that it symbolizes unfulfilled emotions.

The Science student starts calculating the exact percentage full.

The Engineering student goes up to the glass, drinks the scotch and asks, "What's the question?"

A young engineer was leaving the office at 6 p.m. when he found the CEO standing in front of a shredder with a piece of paper in his hand.

"Listen," said the CEO, "this is important, and my secretary has left. Can you make this thing work?"

"Certainly," said the young engineer. He turned the machine on, inserted the paper, and pressed the start button.

"Excellent, excellent!" said the CEO as his paper disappeared inside the machine. "I just need one copy."

There were these two liberal arts students who decided they would go moose hunting in the backwoods of British Columbia. As it happened, they lucked out and got a moose. Unfortunately, they were about a mile from their truck. They were having a tough time dragging the animal by the hind legs when an engineer happened upon them.

He said, "You know, the hair follicles on a moose have a grain to them that causes the hair to lie toward the back. The way you are dragging that moose, it increases your coefficient of friction by a huge margin. If you grab it by the antlers and pull, you will find the work required to be quite minimal."

The liberal arts students thanked him and started dragging

the moose by the antlers. After about an hour, one said, "I can't believe how easy it is to move this moose this way. I sure am glad we ran across that engineer."
"Yeah.", said the other. "But we're getting further and further away from our truck."

Press button to test.
Release to detonate.

A mechanical engineer builds weapons.
A civil engineer builds targets.

Undetectable errors are infinite in number.

Warning! I still have a slide rule and I know how to use it!

One day, and engineer comes up to the gates of hell. The Devil takes a look at him and says, "Well, we've never had an engineer in hell before, but I guess we can take you in." So the engineer goes in.
After a few days, he comes up to the Devil and says, "I'm sure you've noticed, but it's really hot down here! What do you think of setting up a couple of refrigeration coils, getting an icebox set up so we could have iced drinks down here?" Now, the Devil hears this and says, "Why not? If you can set it up, go for it!"
So the engineer gets some tools together, works for a little bit, and sets up his little ice cube maker, and soon the engineer, the Devil, and everyone else is enjoying ice cubes in their drinks, and everyone thinks it's a great improvement. Couple of days later, the engineer comes back to the Devil and says, "Well, I'm impressed by how big Hell is - there are so many people here! But it takes so long to get from place to place - how about I install some people-movers? I can put in escalators, elevators, moving ramps, the works!" The Devil takes a sip of his ice margarita, and says, "Sure, give it a shot." As the engineer works, the souls in Hell start getting around easier - there are elevators, escalators, all sorts of people-

movers! It gets to be quite convenient to get around Hell. After that project, the engineer comes up to the Devil and says, "I've been thinking about tackling the heat down here - ice drinks are all well and good, but it's still bloody hot! How about it?" The Devil at this point returns, "Anything you need, you got it!"

Two weeks later, the first stage of the cooling system goes on-line, and all the damned souls breath a sigh of relief as the heat wave finally breaks. At this point, God comes down to talk to the Devil, and tells him there's been a mistake: "That engineer you've got doesn't belong in Hell - he was meant for Heaven!"

Now, the Devil wasn't about to let his first engineer go! He returns, "Oh, come on - once he's in those gates, he's Mine! That's the way it works, and you know it!"

God tells him, "Well, you're just gonna have to return him! If you don't, I'll, I'll - I'll sue you, is what I'll do!"

The Devil knows he's won - he leans back, cocky as all hell, and asks, "Now, where you gonna find a Lawyer in Heaven?"

How many [IBM] Technical Writers does it take to change a light bulb?

A1: 100. Ten to do it, and 90 to write document number GC7500439-0001, Multitasking Incandescent Source System Facility, of which 10% of the pages state only "This page intentionally left blank", and 20% of the definitions are of the form "...... consists of sequences of non-blank characters separated by blanks".

A2: Just one, provided there's an engineer around to explain how to do it.

A pastor, a doctor and an engineer were waiting one morning for a particularly slow group of golfers. The engineer fumed, "What's with these guys? We must have been waiting for 15 minutes!"

The doctor chimed in, "I don't know, but I've never seen such ineptitude!"

The pastor said, "Hey, here comes the greens keeper. Let's have a word with him."

"Hi George! Say, what's with that group ahead of us? They're rather slow, aren't they?"

The greens keeper replied, "Oh, yes, that's a group of blind firefighters. They lost their sight saving our clubhouse from a fire last year, so we always let them play for free anytime."

The group was silent for a moment. The pastor said, "That's so sad. I think I will say a special prayer for them tonight."

The doctor said, "Good idea. And I'm going to contact my ophthalmologist buddy and see if there's anything he can do for them."

The engineer said, "Why can't these guys play at night?"

The graduate with a Science degree asks, "Why does it work?"

The graduate with an Engineering degree asks, "How does it work?"

The graduate with an Accounting degree asks, "How much will it cost?"

The graduate with an Arts degree asks, "Do you want fries with that?"

An architect, an artist and an engineer were discussing whether it was better to spend time with the wife or a mistress. The architect said he enjoyed time with his wife, building a solid foundation for an enduring relationship. The artist said he enjoyed time with his mistress, because of the passion and mystery he found there. The engineer said, "I like both."

"Both?"

"Yeah. If you have a wife and a mistress, they will each assume you are spending time with the other woman, and you can go to the lab and get some work done."

An engineer was crossing a road one-day when a frog called out to him and said, "If you kiss me, I'll turn into a beautiful princess."

He bent over, picked up the frog and put it in his pocket.

The frog spoke up again and said, "If you kiss me and turn me back into a beautiful princess, I will stay with you for one year."

The engineer took the frog out of his pocket, smiled at it and returned it to the pocket. The frog then cried out, "If you kiss me and turn me back into a princess, I'll stay with you and do ANYTHING you want."

Again the engineer took the frog out, smiled at it and put it back into his pocket. Finally, the frog asked, "What is the matter? I've told you I'm a beautiful princess, and that I'll stay with you for a year and do anything you want. Why won't you kiss me?"

The engineer said, "Look, I'm an engineer. I don't have time for a girlfriend, but a talking frog, now that's cool."

The toilet paper holders in Engineering at CalTech are all inscribed, "Pull here for an Arts Degree - Wipe for honours.

An engineering student, a physics student, and a mathematics student were each given $150 and were told to use the money to find out exactly how tall a particular hotel was.

All three ran off, extremely keen on how to do this.

The physics student went out, purchased some stopwatches, a number of ball bearings, a calculator, and got some friends. He had them all time the drop of ball bearings from the roof, and he then figured out the height from the time it took for the bearings to accelerate from rest until they impacted with the sidewalk.

The math student waited until the sun was going down, then she took out her protractor, plumb line, measuring tape, and scratch pad, measured the length of the shadow, found the angle the building's roof made from the ground, and used trigonometry to figure out the height of the building.

These two students bumped into the engineering student the next day, who was nursing a really bad hangover. When asked what he did to find the height of the building he replied: "Well, I walked up to the bell hop, gave him 10 bucks, asked him how tall the hotel was, and hit the bar inside for happy hour!"

For every simple solution there are numerous complex problems.

A mechanical, electrical, and civil engineer are discussing God.
The M.E. says, "God must be a mechanical engineer! Look at the bones and muscles of the human body! It is a marvelous machine!"
The E.E. says, "No! God is an electrical engineer. Look at the nervous system. It is a miraculous electrical computing system!."
The C.E . says, "You are both wrong. God is a civil engineer. Who else would put a waste facility next to an entertainment complex?"

Four geeks are walking on a beach... ...a med student, a physicist, a mathematician and a mechanical engineer.
They are enjoying their day out when they see a crowd of people crouching around a woman who is lying motionless on the sand. Their geek-curiosity is instantly aroused, and they jog over to investigate.
"What's up?", the med student asks.
"She got caught in the undertow, looks like she's drowned good", one of the crowd answers.
"I think I see a pulse in her temple!" cries the med student, "Quickly, men! Determined action may save her yet!"
The physicist takes off his backpack and from it produces his trusty super soaker. It is the work of a few seconds to fashion it into an effective water pump.
"With this we can empty her lungs of water in no time!", cried the physicist.
The team set to work, and apply the device to her mouth, with the med student and physicist pumping away.
"Keep going men!", the med student encouraged his friends "I think we're winning!".

Minutes pass. Water continues to be pumped from the woman, mixed with sand, shells and candy wrappers. "Remarkable" says the mathematician. By my calculations, they have removed enough water from that woman to fill a cylinder six feet long and two feet in diameter. Most remarkable!".

More minutes pass, and water is still being pumped from the woman.

The med student is beginning to get disheartened: "I'm afraid we're losing her, fellas. She seems to contain more water than I ever thought possible. What time is it - for the records?".

The engineer shakes his head and finally speaks: "Just move her over there," he says indicating a patch of sand about ten feet yonder "and keep pumping".

His colleagues are astounded by the audacity of this suggestion. "How can that affect the amount of water in her body?", asked the med student a touch tetchily.

"Because she's sitting in a puddle , dumbass", replied the engineer.

A philosophy professor stood before his class and had some items in front of him. When the class began, wordlessly he picked up a large empty mayonnaise jar and proceeded to fill it with rocks, rocks about 2" in diameter. He then asked the students if the jar was full. They agreed that it was.

So the professor then picked up a box of pebbles and poured them into the jar. He shook the jar lightly. The pebbles, of course, rolled into the open areas between the rocks. He then asked the students again if the jar was full. They agreed it was.

The professor picked up a box of sand and poured it into the jar. Of course, the sand filled up everything else. "Now," said the professor, "I want you to recognize that this is your life. The rocks are the important things - your family, your partner, your health, your children - things that if everything else was lost and only they remained, your life would still be full. The pebbles are the other things that matter like your job, your house, your car. The sand is everything else. The small stuff."

"If you put the sand into the jar first, there is no room for the pebbles or the rocks. The same goes for your life. If you spend all your time and energy on the small stuff, you will never have room for the things that are important to you. Pay attention to the things that are critical to your happiness. Play with your children. Take time to get medical checkups. Take your partner out dancing. There will always be time to go to work, clean the house, give a dinner party and fix the disposal."

"Take care of the rocks first - the things that really matter. Set your priorities. The rest is just sand."

But then... an engineering student then took the jar which the other students and the professor agreed was full, and proceeded to pour in a glass of beer. Of course the beer filled the remaining spaces within the jar making the jar truly full. The moral of this tale is: no matter how full your life is, there is always room for beer.

There was an engineer who had an exceptional gift for fixing all things mechanical. After serving his company loyally for over 30 years, he happily retired. Several years later the company contacted him regarding a seemingly impossible problem they were having with one of their multimillion dollar machines.

They had tried everything and everyone else to get the machine to work but to no avail. In desperation, they called on the retired engineer who had solved so many of their problems in the past.

The engineer reluctantly took the challenge. He spent a day studying the huge machine. At the end of the day, he marked a small "x" in chalk on a particular component of the machine and stated, "This is where your problem is".

The part was replaced and the machine worked perfectly again.

The company received a bill for $50,000 from the engineer for his service. They demanded an itemized accounting of his charges.

The engineer responded briefly: One chalk mark $1 Knowing where to put it $49,999 It was paid in full and the engineer retired again in peace.

John, an engineer at a manufacturing company, was well respected for his engineering knowledge. When a new computer system was put in to help with the engineering duties, the brass at the company was given a demonstration of the new systems abilities. To give the computer as test, the brass asked the computer a solve a difficult engineering equation. The computer promptly responded back with the perfect answer, "Ask John

Normal people ... believe that if it ain't broke, don't fix it. Engineers believe that if it ain't broke, it doesn't have enough features yet.

A rocket scientist was interviewing professionals to be sent to Mars. Only one could go, but with one catch - he couldn't return to Earth. The first applicant, an engineer, was asked how much he wanted to be paid for going. "One million dollars," he answered, "because I want to donate it to M.I.T." The next applicant, a doctor, was asked the same question. He asked for two million. "I want to give a million to my family and a million to my church."
The last applicant was a lawyer. When asked how much money he wanted, he whispered in the interviewer's ear, "Three million dollars."
"Why so much more than the others?" the interviewer queried.
"Because if I get $3 million, I'll give you $1 million, I'll keep $1 million, and we'll send the engineer."

The Board of Trustees of a nearby University, decides to test the Professors, to see if they really know their stuff. First they take a Math Prof. and put him in a room. Now, the room contains a table and three metal spheres about the size of softballs. They tell him to do whatever he want with the balls and the table in one hour. After an hour, he comes out and the Trustees look in and the balls are arranged in a triangle at the center of the table. Next, they give the same test to a Physics Prof. After an hour, they look in, and the balls are stacked one on top of the other in the center of the table. Finally, they give the test to an Engineering Prof. After an hour, they look in and one of the balls is broken, one is missing, and he's carrying the third out in his lunchbox.

ATMs FOR ENGINEERS:
1. Load the card into the transverse slot at 46 degrees south.
2. Affix the numerical sequence into the keypad to confirm coordinates.
3. Choose the variated differentiations:
a) Longitudinal transference of cash
b) Contraction variance from your account
c) Separation of spouse's credit card from principal turbine producer
d) Visual mathematical calculation of account balance telemetry.
4. Dislodgement of card is required.
5. Remove the crystallization by-products.
6. Project completed. Turn your structure 94 degrees with differential allowance of 0.4925 and mobilize yourself out of here.

A programmer and an engineer were sitting next to each other on an airplane. The programmer leans over to the engineer and asks if he wants to play a fun game. The engineer just wants to sleep so he politely declines, turns away, and tries to sleep. The programmer persists and explains that it's a real easy game. He explains, "I'll ask a question and if you don't know the answer you pay me $5. Then you ask me a question and if I don't know the answer I'll pay you $5." Again, the engineer politely declines and tries to sleep.
The programmer, now somewhat agitated, says, "OK, if you

don't know the answer, you pay me $5, and if I don't know the answer, I'll pay you $50!" Now, that got the engineer's attention, so he agrees to the game. The programmer asks the first question, "What is the distance from the earth to the moon?" The engineer doesn't say a word and just hands the programmer $5.

Now, it's the engineer's turn. He asks the programmer, "What goes up a hill with three legs and comes down on four?" The programmer looks at him with a puzzled look, takes out his laptop computer, looks through all his references and after about an hour wakes the engineer and hands him $50. The engineer politely takes the $50, turns away, and tries to return to sleep.

The programmer, a little miffed, asks, "Well? What's the answer to the question?" Without a word, the engineer reaches into his wallet, hands $5 to the programmer and returns to sleep.

Arguing with an engineer is a lot like wrestling in the mud with a pig.
After a few hours, you realize that he likes it.

An astronaut in space in 1970 was asked by a reporter, "How do you feel?"
"How would you feel," the astronaut replied, "if you were stuck here, on top of 20,000 parts each one supplied by the lowest engineering bidder?

An engineer learned shortly before quitting time that he had to attend a meeting. He tried unsuccessfully to locate his car-pool members to let them know that he would not be leaving with them. Hastily he scribbled a message to one fellow and left it on his desk: "Last-minute meeting. Leave without me. Ted."
At 6:30 p.m., the engineer stopped at his desk and found this note: "Meet us at the bar and grill across the street. You drove."

A successful engineer flew to Vegas for the weekend to gamble. He lost the shirt off his back, and had nothing left but a quarter and the second half of his round trip ticket. If he could just get to the airport he could get himself home. So he went out to the front of the casino where there was a cab waiting. He got in and explained his situation to the cabbie. He promised to send the driver money from home, he offered him his credit card numbers, his driver's license number, his address, etc. but to no avail. The cabbie said (adopt appropriate dialect), "If you don't have fifteen dollars, get the hell out of my cab!" So the businessman was forced to hitchhike to the airport and was barely in time to catch his flight.

One year later the engineer, having worked long and hard to regain his financial success, returned to Vegas and this time he won big. Feeling pretty good about himself, he went out to the front of the casino to get a cab ride back to the airport. Well who should he see out there, at the end of a long line of cabs, but his old buddy who had refused to give him a ride when he was down on his luck. The engineer thought for a moment about how he could make the guy pay for his lack of charity, and he hit on a plan.

The engineer got in the first cab in the line, "How much for a ride to the airport," he asked? "Fifteen bucks," came the reply.

"And how much for you to go down on me during the way?"

"What?! Get out, out of my cab, you scum."

The engineer got into the back of each cab in the long line and asked the same questions, with the same result - getting kicked out of each taxi.

When he got to his old friend at the back of the line, he got in and asked "How much for a ride to the airport?"

The cabbie replied "Fifteen bucks."

The engineer said "O.K." and off they went. Then, as they drove slowly past the long line of cabs the engineer gave a big smile and a big thumbs up.

There were three engineers in a car; an electrical engineer, a chemical engineer, and a Microsoft engineer.
Suddenly, the car stops running and they pull off to the side of the road wondering what could be wrong.
The electrical engineer suggests stripping down the electronics of the car and trying to trace where a fault may have occurred.
The chemical engineer, not knowing much about cars, suggests maybe the fuel is becoming emulsified and getting blocked somewhere.
The Microsoft engineer, not knowing much about anything, came up with a suggestion. "Why don't we close all the windows, get out, get back in, and open all the windows and see if it works?"

One day, an engineer and a mathematician walk around and meet a very rich man who tells them that if they can get all the way over to it, they are allowed to take the sack, filled with gold, standing on the ground 20 m away. However, they are only allowed to take steps of a length of maximum half the remaining distance. The mathematician knows it isn't possible to get to the sack on these conditions, so he does nothing. Then the engineer walks all the way to the sack with normal sized steps, grabs the sack, and walks back.
"But..." says the mathematician, "... how...?"
"Measurement insecurity!" says the engineer.

During the heat of the space race in the 1960's, NASA decided it needed a ball point pen to write in the zero gravity confines of its space capsules.
After considerable research and development, the Astronaut Pen was developed at a cost of $1 million. The pen worked and also enjoyed some modest success as a novelty item back here on earth.
The Soviet Union, when faced with the same problem, used a pencil.

A group of sales and marketing experts were given the assignment of measuring the height of a flagpole. Wearing suits and ties, they marched out to the flagpole with their ladders and tape measures, falling all over themselves to get an accurate reading.

An engineer comes along and sees what they're trying to do. He walks over, pulls the flagpole out of the ground, lays it flat on the ground, measures it from end to end, gives the measurement to one of the so-called experts, puts the pole back vertically into its slot in the ground and walks away. After the engineer has gone, the sales guy turns to a marketing guy and laughs. "Isn't that just like an engineer?" he says. "We're looking for the height, and he gives us the length!"

A rather inhibited engineer finally splurged on a luxury cruise to the Caribbean. It was the "craziest" thing he had ever done in his life.

Just as he was beginning to enjoy himself, a hurricane roared upon the huge ship, capsizing it like a child's toy. Somehow, the engineer, desperately hanging on to a life preserver, managed to wash ashore on a secluded island.
Outside of the beautiful scenery, a spring-fed pool, bananas and coconuts, there was little else. He lost all hope and for hours on end, sat under the same palm tree. One day, after several months had passed, a gorgeous woman in a small rowboat appeared.
"I'm from the other side of the island," she said. "Were you on the cruise ship too?"
"Yes, I was," he answered. "But where did you get the rowboat?"
"Well, I whittled the oars from the gum tree branches, wove the reinforced gunnel from palm branches, and made the keel and stern from a eucalyptus tree."
"But, what did you use for tools?" asked the man.
"There was a very unusual strata of alluvial rock exposed on the south side of the island. I discovered that if I fired it to a

certain temperature in my kiln, it melted into ductile iron. Anyhow, that's how I got the tools. But enough of that," she said. "Where have you been living all this time? I don't see any shelter."

"To be honest, I've just been sleeping on the beach."

"Would you like to come to my place?" the woman asked. The engineer nodded dumbly. She expertly rowed them around to her side of the island, and tied up the boat with a handsome strand of hand-woven hemp topped with a neat back splice. They walked up a winding stone walk she had laid around a palm tree. There stood an exquisite bungalow painted in blue and white.

"It's not much, but I call it home." Inside, she said, "Sit down please; would you like a drink?"

"No thanks," said the man. "One more coconut juice and I'll throw up!"

"It won't be coconut juice," the woman replied. "I have a crude still out back, so we can have authentic Pina Coladas." Trying to hide his amazement, the man accepted the drink, and they sat down on her couch to talk. After they had exchanged stories, the woman asked, "Tell me, have you always had a beard?"

"No," the man replied, "I was clean shaven all of my life until I ended up on this island."

"Well, if you'd like to shave, there's a razor upstairs in the bathroom cabinet."

The man, no longer questioning anything, went upstairs to the bathroom and shaved with an intricate bone-and-shell device honed razor sharp. Next he showered-- not even attempting to fathom a guess as to how she managed to get warm water into the bathroom-- and went back downstairs. He couldn't help but admire the masterfully carved banister as he walked.

"You look great," said the woman. "I think I'll go upstairs and slip into something more comfortable." As she did, the man continued to sip his Pina Colada. After a short time, the woman, smelling faintly of gardenias, returned, wearing a revealing gown fashioned out of pounded palm fronds.

"Tell me," she asked, "we've both been out here for a very

long time with no companionship. You know what I mean. Haven't you been lonely too? Isn't there something that you really, really miss? Something that all men and women need? Something that would be really nice to have right now?!"

"Yes there is!" the man replied, shucking off his shyness. "There is something I've wanted to do for so long. But on this island all alone, it was just, well... impossible."

"Well, it's not impossible any more," the woman said.

The man, practically panting in excitement, said breathlessly, "You mean... you actually figured out some way we can check our e-mail?!"

An enthusiastic but somewhat unscrupulous salesman was waiting to see the purchasing agent of an engineering firm. The salesman was there to submit his company's bid, or price quote, for a particular job. He couldn't help but notice, however, that a competitor's bid was on the purchasing agent's desk. Unfortunately, the actual figure was covered by a juice can. The temptation to see the amount quoted became too much, and the salesman reached over and lifted the can. His heart sank as he watched thousands of BB pellets pour from the bottomless can and scatter across the floor.

There once was a dog show to determine the world's smartest dog. Three dogs were in the finals. One dog belonged to a doctor. One dog belonged to an engineer. And, one dog belonged to a lawyer. For the finals each dog was given a bag of bones to see what it could make.

The doctor said, "Stethoscope, go!" The dog built a human skeleton. The judges were ready to award the trophy right then. But, they decided to give the other dogs a try.

The engineer said, "Slide-rule, go!" (So, its an old joke.) The dog built a suspension bridge. The judges were beside themselves. Which dog would they pick?

The lawyer said. "Loop-hole, go!" The dog ate the bones, got a percentage of all the tolls from the bridge and screwed the other two dogs.

An engineer, a psychologist, and a theologian were hunting in the wilderness of northern Canada. Suddenly, the temperature dropped and a furious snowstorm was upon them. They came across an isolated cabin, far removed from any town. The hunters had heard that the locals in the area were quite hospitable, so they knocked on the door to ask permission to rest.

No one answered their knocks, but they discovered the cabin was unlocked and they entered. It was a simple place, two rooms with a minimum of furniture and household equipment. Nothing was unusual about the cabin except the stove. It was large, pot-bellied, and made of cast-iron. What was strange about it was its location. It was suspended in midair by wires attached to the ceiling beams.

"Fascinating," said the psychologist. "It is obvious that this lonely trapper, isolated from humanity, has elevated this stove so that he can curl up under it and vicariously experience a return to the womb."

"Nonsense!" replied the engineer. "The man is practicing the laws of thermodynamics. By elevating his stove, he has discovered a way to distribute heat more evenly throughout the cabin."

"With all due respect," interrupted the theologian, "I'm sure that hanging his stove from the ceiling has religious meaning. Fire lifted up has been a religious symbol for centuries."

The three debated the point for several hours without resolving the issue. When the trapper finally returned, they immediately asked him why he had hung his heavy pot-bellied stove from the ceiling.

His answer was succinct. "Had plenty of wire, not much stove pipe."

The engineer concluded his lecture with a note of caution. "You don't want to try these techniques at home."

"Why not?" asked someone from the back of the audience.

"I watched my wife's routine at breakfast for years," the engineer explained. "She made lots of trips to the refrigerator, stove, table and cabinets, often carrying just a

single item at a time. 'Hon,' I suggested, 'Why don't you try carrying several things at once?'"
The voice from the back asked, "Did it save time?"
The engineer replied, "Actually, yes. It used to take her 20 minutes to get breakfast ready. Now I do it in seven."

A promising young NASA aerospace engineer was killed in a horrific car accident and arrived in Heaven, protesting to St. Peter at the pearly gates. "St. Peter, I'm only 35. I'm much too young to die. I have a wonderful wife and family, so much to live for. Why in the world am I here?"
St. Peter looked through a huge stack of papers, looked over the top of his glasses and said, "Well, according to all of these hours on your time sheets, you've got to be at least 108."

Three engineers were in a bar and spotted a hydrogeologist. They decided to have fun with the man.
One of the engineers walked over to the hydrogeologist, tapped him on the shoulder, and said, "Hey, I hear your Henry Darcy was a girly-man."
"Oh really, hmm, didn't know that," said the hydrogeologist. Puzzled, the engineer walked back to his buddies. "I told him Henry Darcy was a girly-man, and he didn't care."
The second engineer remarked, "You just don't know how to set him off...watch and learn." So, the second engineer walked over to the hydrogeologist, tapped him on the shoulder and said, "Hey, I hear your Henry Darcy was a transvestite!"
"Oh really, hmm, didn't know that."
Shocked beyond belief, the engineer went back to his buddies. "You're right. He's unshakable!"
The third engineer remarked, "Boys, I'll really tick him off...just watch." So the third engineer walked over to the hydrogeologist, tapped him on the shoulder and said, "I hear Henry Darcy was an engineer!"
"Yeah, that's what your buddies were trying to tell me."

Dilbert is a documentary.

Back in the 60's, a jet manufacturer was trying to build a jet that would go mach 4 (4 times the speed of sound for you non-aeronautical types). Finally after many years of design, the jet was finished. A test pilot took it out for it's maiden flight. Everyone gathered around ... and the plane went to Mach1 ... Mach2 ... Mach3 ... Mach3.5 ... and the wings ripped off, the plan hit the ground and killed the test pilot.

The engineers went back to the design and spent months re-vamping it. They came out with the new and improved second version, but when they tested it, it had the same disastrous results: the plane's wings ripped off and the pilot was killed in the crash.   The engineers went through 7 iterations, until finally they were about to give up. They decided to contact Bob, a retired engineer with the reputation of being able to fix all problems.

Bob comes in, asks to see all the design figures, charts, and drawings, and takes them home to study them. He calls the next day and says he has discovered a solution to the problem: drill holes vertically through the wings at the exact spot where they attach to the body.

At first everyone argues - the wings are ripping off now, why drill holes to them? but Bob insists that it will work. So eventually, they give in and do it. The jet is tested later that day and not only does it reach Mach4, but it goes to Mach5.3 before the test is declared over and successful. All the engineers rush to Bob and congratulate him for his uncanny ability to discover the solution. "How did you know?" asks one of the engineers.

 "Well, I'll tell you. I was on the toilet, and it occurred to me - toilet paper never tears on the perforations."

Question: What is the sum of 2 + 2

An accountant will say "What do you want the answer to be?"

A mathematician will say "I believe it is 4, but I will have to prove it."

A statistician will say "The population is too small to give an accurate answer, but on the basis of the data supplied the answer lies between 3 and 5."

An economist will say "Based on today's thinking, the answer is 4 but the answer may be different tomorrow".
An engineer will say "The answer is 4, but adding a safety factor we will call it 5"

There was once an engineer who found a magic lamp. When he rubbed it, a genie jumped out and said to him, "You have three wishes. But there is a catch - this wish system of mine was designed by a lawyer, so whatever you wish for every lawyer in the world will get double of!"
The engineer replied, "That's no problem, I can live with that." He then said, "For my first wish, I wish I had a Ferarri."
"OK", said the genie, and a Ferarri appeared in front of the engineer. "But remember, every lawyer in the world now has 2 Ferarris," the genie told the engineer.
The engineer remained unperturbed and said, "For my second wish, I wish for a million bucks."
So a million bucks appeared in front of the engineer and the genie said, "Remember, every lawyer in the world now has 2 million bucks."
The engineer was non-committal and then said, "I always wished I could donate a kidney!"

An accountant, a lawyer, and an engineer were supervising construction work on the 20th floor of a building. They were eating lunch and the accountant said, "Corned beef and cabbage! If I get corned beef and cabbage one more time for lunch I'm going to jump off this building."
The lawyer opened his lunch box and exclaimed, "Burritos again! If I get burritos one more time I'm going to jump off, too."
The engineer opened his lunch and said, "Bologna again. If I get a bologna sandwich one more time I'm jumping too."
Next day - the accountant opens his lunch box, sees corned beef and cabbage and jumps to his death. The lawyer open his lunch, sees a burrito and jumps too. The engineer opens his lunch, sees the bologna and jumps to his death also.
At the funeral - The accountant's wife is weeping. She says,

"If I'd known how really tired he was of corned beef and cabbage I never would have given it to him again!"
The lawyer's wife also weeps and says "I could have given him tacos or enchiladas! I didn't realize he hated burritos so much."
Everyone turned and stared at the engineer's wife. "Hey, don't look at me," she said, "He makes his own lunch!"

What do you get when you cross an engineer with a woodwind player?
Someone with three piccolos, a flute, and two clarinets in his shirt pocket.

When considering the behavior of a howitzer:
A mathematician will be able to calculate where the shell will land.
A physicist will be able to explain how the shell gets there.
An engineer will stand there and try to catch it.

A mathematician, scientist, and engineer are each asked:
"Suppose we define a horse's tail to be a leg. How many legs does a horse have?"
The mathematician answers "5"; the scientist "1"; and the engineer says, "But you can't do that!"

If it wasn't for Thomas Alva Edison, we'd all be watching TV to the light of a candle.

A friend of mine has a theory about things electronic: they operate on smoke. It is very important for each component to have the correct amount of smoke, which is sealed inside at the factory. If this smoke ever gets out, the part is no longer functional.
This is true: how many times have you ever seen an electrical or electronic device work right after smoke has been emitted?

The great mathematician John Von Neumann was consulted by a group who was building a rocket ship to send into outer space. When he saw the incomplete structure, he asked, "Where did you get the plans for this ship?"

He was told, "We have our own staff of engineers."

He disdainfully replied: "Engineers! Why, I have completely sewn up the whole mathematical theory of rocketry. See my paper of 1952."

Well, the group consulted the 1952 paper, completely scrapped their 10 million dollar structure, and rebuilt the rocket exactly according to Von Neumann's plans. The minute they launched it, the entire structure blew up. They angrily called Von Neumann back and said: "We followed your instructions to the letter. Yet when we started it, it blew up! Why?"

Von Neumann replied, "Ah, yes; that is technically known as the blow-up problem - I treated that in my paper of 1954."

Top 25 Engineering Terms and Expressions (What they say and what they really
mean)

Customer satisfaction is believed to be assured. (We're so far behind schedule that the customer will settle for anything.)

Please see me / Let's discuss it. (I need your help. I've screwed up again.)

The project is in process. (It's so tied up in red tape that it's completely hopeless.)

We're trying a number of different approaches. (We still guessing, at this point.)

We're following the standard. (We've always done it this way.)

Close project coordination. (We met together and had coffee.)

Years of development. (It finally worked.)

Energy saving. (Turn off the power to save electricity.)

We'll have to abandon the entire concept. (The only person who understood the thing just quit.)

We had a major technological breakthrough. (It's boring, but it looks high tech.)

We're preparing a report with a fresh approach. (We just hired a couple of kids out of college.)

Preliminary operational tests proved inconclusive. (It blew up when we flipped the switch.)

Test results proved extremely gratifying. (Yahoo! It actually worked.)

Please read and initial. (We want to spread around the responsibility.)

Tell us what you are thinking. (We'll listen, but if it disagrees with what we've already done or are planning to do, forget it.)

Tell us your interpretation. (Let's hear your bull.)

We'll look into it. (Forget it! We've got so many other problems already, we'll never get to it.)

No maintenance. (If it breaks, we can't fix it.)

Low maintenance. (If it breaks, we're no likely able to fix it.)

All new. (None of the parts are interchangeable with the previous design.)

Rugged. (Needs major equipment to lift it.)

Robust. (More than rugged.)

Light weight. (A little less than rugged.)

Fax it to me. (I'm too lazy to write it down.)

I haven't gotten your email. (It's been days since I've checked my email.)

HOW CAN YOU TELL IF YOUR CHILD IS GOING TO BE AN ENGINEER?

Watch for these tell-tale warning signs:

You buy your child an educational software program, and she asks which authoring tool it was written in.

Your child has torn apart his teddy bear and is studying the chemical composition of the filling.

She can program you VCR, while you haven't been able to get it to stop blinking "12:00."

He has removed the voice box from his Talking Elmo doll and reprogrammed it to recite the periodic table.

She has replaced the arms and legs of her Barbie Doll with bionic limbs.

He is picked last on every sports team.

You take her to see Disney's "Hunchback of Notre Dame," and all she's interested in is the computer animation.

He has Bill Gates posters in his room.

She believes that if she's really good, Santa will give her a client/server network for Christmas.

He throws a temper tantrum every time you refuse to take him into Fry's.

She has accepted a scholarship to MIT. And she's five.

He gets in fights in school because he owns a PC and the other kids use a Mac.

She can't get a date.

He has defeated the "child-guard" software on your Web browser and has connected to www.playboy.com.

Forget Dr. Seuss and Beatrix Potter. She wants you to read her Carl Sagan.

When he is asked to play the Star of Bethlehem in the Christmas pageant, he asks, "Am I a white dwarf or red giant?"

How Engineers Do It

Engineers do it with precision.
Electrical engineers are shocked when they do it.
Electrical engineers do it on an impulse.
Electrical engineers do it with large capacities.
Electrical engineers do it with more frequency and less resistance.
Electrical engineers do it with more power and at higher frequency.
 Mechanical engineers do it with stress and strain.
Mechanical engineers do it with less energy and greater efficiency.
Chemical Engineers do it in fluidized beds.
City planners do it with their eyes closed.

How many engineers does it take to change a light bulb?
A1: None. They are all too busy trying to design the perfect light bulb.
A2: Only the one with the instruction manual.
A3: One. But she would insist that the way she did it was distinctive.
A4: Three. One to hold the ladder, one to hold the light bulb, and the third to interpret the Japanese text.
A5: Five. One to design a nuclear-powered light bulb that never needs changing, one to figure out how to power the rest of the USA using that nuked light bulb, two to install it, and one to write the computer program that controls the wall switch.

How many first year engineering students does it take to change a light bulb?
None. That's a second year subject.

How many second year engineering students does it take to change a light bulb?
One, but the rest of the class copies the report.

How many third year engineering students does it take to change a light bulb?
"Will this question be on the final exam?"

How many civil engineers does it take to change a light bulb?
Two. One to do it and one to steady the chandelier.

How many electrical engineers does it take to change a light bulb?
None. They simply redefine darkness as the industry standard.

How many computer engineers does it take to change a light bulb?
"Why bother? The socket will be obsolete in six months anyway."

How many mechanical engineers does it take to change a light bulb?
Five. One to decide which way the bulb ought to turn, one to calculate the force required, one to design a tool with which to turn the bulb, one to design a comfortable-but functional-hand grip, and one to use all this equipment.

How many nuclear engineers does it take to change a light bulb?
Seven. One to install the new bulb and six to figure out what to do with the old one.

REAL ENGINEERS... · Real Engineers consider themselves well dressed if their socks match.
· Real Engineers buy their spouses a set of matched screwdrivers for their birthday.
· Real Engineers wear mustaches or beards for "efficiency".

Not because they're lazy.
· Real engineers have a non-technical vocabulary of 800 words.
· Real Engineers think a "biting wit" is their fox terrier.
· Real Engineers know the second law of thermodynamics - but not their own shirt size.
· Real Engineers repair their own cameras, telephones, televisions, watches, and automatic transmissions.
· Real Engineers say "It's 70 degrees Fahrenheit, 25 degrees Celsius, and 298 degrees Kelvin" and all you say is "Isn't it a nice day"
· Real Engineers give you the feeling you're having a conversation with a dial tone or busy signal.
· Real Engineers wear badges so they don't forget who they are. Sometimes a note is attached saying "Don't offer me a ride today. I drove my own car".
· Real Engineers' politics run towards acquiring a parking space with their name on it and an office with a window.
· Real Engineers know the "ABC's of Infrared" from A to B.
· Real Engineers rotate their tires for laughs.
· Real Engineers will make four sets of drawings (with seven revisions) before making a bird bath.
· Real Engineers' briefcases contain a Phillips screwdriver, a copy of "Quantum Physics", and a half of a peanut butter sandwich.
· Real Engineers don't find the above at all funny.

OLD ENGINEERS never die, they just lose their bearings
OLD ELECTRICAL ENGINEERS never die, they just have slower rise times
OLD ELECTRICIANS never die, they just do it until it Hz
OLD ELECTRICIANS never die, they just lose contact

YOU MAY BE AN ENGINEER...
If you refer to your spouse as "\woman at home.wife,"
If your favorite TV show is "Mr. Wizard" instead of "Baywatch,"

If when your family is expecting, you are more interested in the ultra-sound equipment than the test results,

If when someone asks "What's new?" you answer "C over lambda,"

If you know Bill Gates' e-mail address, and don't remember your own,

If you are always asking your friends from marketing to hold two leads to a giant capacitor,

If you find your head nodding up and down every time you read Dilbert,

If your pocket is full of too many mechanical pencils,

If when your 3-year old asks "Why is the sky blue?" you start explaining it to them,

If you can explain which direction the water spins as you flush the toilet and why,

If you go to the air show, and you start calculating how fast the sky divers are falling, you may be an engineer; if you start telling all the people around you, you definitely are.

If you need a spreadsheet to figure out who owes what for lunch,

If you plan your family vacation on a Gantt chart,

If you pre-plan your route on a map of the exhibits through the annual computer show at Moscone Center,

If you read PC World and Popular Mechanics while on vacation,

If you are willing to debate for two hours the possible results of an experiment that takes five minutes to run,

If you know the altitudes at which you must turn off electronic devices on an airplane, and why,

If on a camping trip, your spouse starts complaining about bug "bites" and you respond that "Yes, we do need more memory in our computer,"

If Dilbert is your hero

If you stare at an orange juice container because it says CONCENTRATE

If you want an 8X CDROM for Christmas

If you can name 6 Star Trek episodes

If the only jokes you receive are through e-mail

If your wrist watch has more computing power than a

486DX2-50

If your idea of good interpersonal communication means getting the decimal point in the right place

If you look forward to Christmas only to put together the kids' toys

If you introduce your wife as "mylady@home.wife"

If your spouse sends you an e-mail instead of calling you to dinner

If you can quote scenes from any Monty Python movie

If you use a CAD package to design your son's Pine Wood Derby car

If you have used coat hangers and duct tape for something other than hanging coats and taping ducts

If, at Christmas, it goes without saying that you will be the one to find the burnt-out bulb in the string

If you window shop at Radio Shack

If your ideal evening consists of fast-forwarding through the latest Sci-Fi movie looking for technical inaccuracies

If you have "Dilbert" comics displayed anywhere in your work area

If you carry on a one-hour debate over the expected results of a test that actually takes five minutes to run

If you are convinced you can build a phazer out of your garage door opener and your camera's flash attachment

If you don't even know where the cover to your personal computer is

If you have modified your can-opener to be microprocessor driven

If you know the direction the water swirls when you flush

If you own "Official Star Trek" anything

If you have ever taken the back off your TV just to see what's inside

If a team of you and your co-workers have set out to modify the antenna on the radio in your work area for better reception

If you ever burned down the gymnasium with your Science Fair project

If you are currently gathering the components to build your own nuclear reactor

If you own one or more white short-sleeve dress shirts

If you have never backed-up your hard drive

If you are aware that computers are actually only good for playing games, but are afraid to say it out loud

If you truly believe aliens are living among us

If you have ever saved the power cord from a broken appliance

If you have ever purchased an electronic appliance "as-is"

If you see a good design and still have to change it

If the salespeople at Circuit City can't answer any of your questions

If you still own a slide rule and you know how to work it

If the thought that a CD could refer to finance or music never enters your mind

If you own a set of itty-bitty screw drivers, but you don't remember where they are

If you rotate your screen savers more frequently than your automobile tires

If you have a functioning home copier machine, but every toaster you own turns bread into charcoal

If you have more toys than your kids

If you need a checklist to turn on the TV

If you have introduced your kids by the wrong name

If you have a habit of destroying things in order to see how they work

If your I.Q. number is bigger than your weight

If the microphone or visual aids at a meeting don't work and you rush up to the front to fix it

If you can remember 7 computer passwords but not your anniversary

If you have memorized the program schedule for the Discovery Channel and have seen most of the shows already

If you have ever owned a calculator with no equal key and know what RPN stands for

If your father sat 2 inches in front of your family's first color TV with a magnifying lens to see how they made the colors, and you grew up thinking that was normal

If you know how to take the cover off of your computer, and what size screw driver to use

If you can type 70 words a minute but can't read your own handwriting

If people groan at the party when you pick out the music=7F

If you can't remember where you parked your car for the 3rd time this week

If you did the sound system for your senior prom

If your checkbook always balances

If your wristwatch has more buttons than a telephone

If you have more friends on the Internet than in real life

If you thought the real heroes of "Apollo 13" were the Mission Controllers

If you think that when people around you yawn, it's because they didn't get enough sleep

If you spend more on your home computer than your car

If you know what http:/ stands for

If you've ever tried to repair a $5.00 radio

If you have a neatly sorted collection of old bolts and nuts in your garage

If your three year old son asks why the sky is blue and you try to explain atmospheric absorption theory

If your lap-top computer costs more than your car

If your 4 basic food groups are: 1. Caffeine 2. Fat 3. Sugar 4. Chocolate

Geology jokes

What did the post doctorate study when he changed fields from particle physics to geology?
Earthquarks.

Does an excellent student of vulcanology graduate magma cum laude?

A man goes into a restaruant, sits down and starts reading the menu.
The menu says:
Broiled Accountant $5.95 per plate
Fried Engineer $7.95 per plate
Toasted Teacher $7.95 per plate
Grilled Geologist $25.95 per plate
The man calls a waiter over and asks "Hey, why does the Grilled Geologist cost so much more?"
The waiter says, " Are you kidding? Do you know how hard it is to clean one of them?

Folds, thrusts, and overturned beds are all common in zones of orogeny

So I was standing in the library discussing cleavage with a female colleague when the topic of intrusive dikes comes up. She said that the dikes she knew of were often associated with thrusting movements in a bed.
I said that I usually didn't associate dikes with any sort of thrusting, but then you never know what can happen when a dike was in an orogenous zone.

How does a geologist get his rocks off?
With a hammer and chisel.

That is the difference between a geologist and a chemist?
A chemist will drink anything that is distilled.
A geologist will drink anything that is fermented.

Why did the fold get arrested?
He was caught rolling a joint!

Two Geologists are walking across a granite outcrop one day.
The first says to the second "Hey, this terrain is
unmetamorphosed".
Replies the second one, "No Schist".

Geologists make the bed rock.
Geographers do it globally.
Geologists are great explorers.
Geologists do it eruptively, with glow, and always smoke
afterwards.
Geologists do it in folded beds.
Geologists do it to get their rocks off.
Geologists know how to make the bedrock.
Geologists do it on the rocks.
Geophysicists do it on impulse
Geophysicists do it with higher frequency.
Geologists have paleomagnetic personalities.
Geophysical exercise.
Geologists never lose their luster.
Geologists don't wrinkle, they show lineation.
Geologists are gneiss people, everyone else is just schist.
Geologists get rock solid when in a sedimentary position.

A pair of geologists are studying terns on a rock island just
off the coast. While walking on a distant part of the island,
they are shot at by a group of thugs operating a pot farm.
This happens several times and the local law enforcement
refuses to investigate. On their last day on the island they
happen into a huge pile of harvested grass that has been set
out to dry. Quickly they decide to set it on fire to pay the

thugs back for shooting at them. The fire takes off and sends plumes of smoke into the sky. As they are running for their boat, they notice that the soaring birds are acting weird, spiraling out of control and crashing into the trees. The next day they read the headlines in the local paper:
Pot Farm Burns - No Tern Left Unstoned.

Why aren't there more geologists?
Most kids grow up !

In California, when a bridge falls down, we know it must be San Andreas' Fault!
A pair of geologists were out doing some field work when they discovered an abandoned well near an old farm house. Of course they're curious so they drop a small stone into the well, but they never hear it hit bottom. They search and find a larger rock and drop it into the well but once again hear nothing. They decide they need something larger and search the farm yard for a larger object. After much struggle, they manage to drag a large railroad tie to the edge of the well and drop it over the edge. After several seconds, a goat tears across the yard and without any hesitation, dives head first into the open hole. The two biologists stand in amazement. About then a farmer appears and tells them he is looking for a lost goat. The biologists tell the farmer about the goat diving into the well.
"That couldn't be my goat", the farmer replies, "My goat was grazing in the field tied to a railroad tie!"

I find drillers boring.

Geologists are good at examining 100 cleavage whilst bedding a slag hoping to be cumming tonite

YOU MIGHT BE A GEOLOGIST IF. . .

You can pronounce the word "molybdenite" correctly on the first try.

You think the primary function of road cuts is tourist attractions.

You own more pieces of quartz than underwear.

You associate the word "hard" with a value on the Mohs scale instead of "work".

The rockpile in your garage is taller than you are.

You have a strong opinion as to whether pieces of concrete are properly called "rocks".

The local university's geology department requests permission to hold field trips in your back yard.

You associate the name "Franklin" with New Jersey instead of "Ben".

There's amethyst in your aquarium.

Your wife has ever had to ask you to move flats of rocks out of the tub so she could take a bath.

Your spelling checker has a vocabulary that includes the words "polymorph" and "pseudomorph".

Your children are named Rocky, Jewel, and Beryl.

You were the only member of the group who spent their time looking at cathedral walls through a pocket magnifier during your trip to Europe.

They won't give you time off from work to attend the Tucson Gem and Mineral Show and you go anyway.

You begin fussing because the light strips you installed on your bookshelves aren't full spectrum.

You've ever purchased an individual, unfaceted rock, regardless of the price.

You've ever spent more than ten dollars for a book about rocks.

You shouted "Obsidian!" to a theater full of movie-goers while watching "The Shawshank Redemption".

The polished slab on your bola tie is six inches in diameter.

You find yourself compelled to examine individual rocks in driveway gravel.

The USGS identifies your collection as a major contributing factor to isostasy in your state.

You know the location of every rock shop within a 100 mile radius of your home.

When they haven't seen you for a week, the shop owners send you get well cards.

You're retired and still thinking of adding another room to your house.

Your idea of a "quiet, romantic evening at home" involves blue mineral   tack and thumbnail boxes.

You're planning on using a pick and shovel while you're on vacation.

You can point out where Tsumeb is on a world globe.

You think Franklin,New Jersey might be a cool place to go on a vacation.

You associate the word "saw" with diamonds instead of "wood".

You begin wondering what a complete set of the Mineralogical Record is worth. When you find out, you actually consider paying it.

You've fabricated a backpack for your dog.

You've installed more than one mineralogical database program on your computer.

The baggage handlers at the airport know you by name and refuse to help
with your luggage.

You receive a letter from the county informing you a landfill permit is required to put anymore rocks on your property.

Your internet home page has pictures of your rocks.

There's a copy of Dana's Manual next to your toilet.

You still think pet rocks are a pretty neat idea.

You get excited when you discover a hardware store that stocks 16 pound sledge hammers and 5 foot long pry bars.

You debate for months on the internet concerning the relative advantages and drawbacks of vibratory verses drum tumblers.

Your employer has asked you not to bring any more rocks to the office   until they have time to reinforce the floor.

You decide not to get married because you'd rather keep the rock.

You judge a restaurant by the type of decorative building stone they use rather than their food.

You manage to turn any conversation into a discussion of geology, as in: "What did you think of that Superbowl game last night?" or "I must have missed that conference. Who sponsored it? Geological Society of America?"

The only thing you notice about attractive members of the opposite sex is the stone in their jewelry.

You refuse to let nightfall stop your field excursions and continue looking at the outcrops using the headlights of your field vehicle.

You like rock music only because it's called "rock" music.

You will try to claw through the water flowing in a stream to get a better look at the bedrock at the base of the channel.

You will walk across eight lanes of freeway traffic to see if the outcrop on the other side of the highway is the same type of rock as the   side you're parked on.

You name your children after rocks and minerals.

You're not sure if you have children.

You view non-geologists as subhuman.

You watch Westerns movies just for the geology.

"Oppressed geology undergrads of the world - CRYSTALIZE!"

I studied geology in college, but found the core curriculum was too deep.

When I took geology, I went through a metamorphosis. I really dig the subject.

Shale I tell you about my college days? I sometimes take them for granite.

Basalt: Salted sheep.

Why are geologists unhappy?
People take them for granite.

What do you call a geologist who doesn't hear anything?
Stone deaf

Upper crust- A lot of crumbs held together with dough.

How did everyone know the volcano was angry?
Because it was fuming.

Why did the geologist win first place in the Braille contest?
Because he had a great feeled test.

What do a geologist and a clairvoyant have in common?
They both are great remote sensing experts.

What state do geologists live in? Ochrehoma.

Why did the geologist get expelled by the School House Marm?
He couldn't keep a clean slate!

Where do geologists like to relax?
In a rocking chair.

Garvin the geologist, was in Alaska studying fault lines. In sub-zero weather, he would spend 7 days out on the coast. But, after his 7 days in the field, he would return to the small town and spend a day or two resting up and drinking in the only bar in town.
On one particular day it was 40 below zero and Garvin made his way into the bar. He asked Bud, the bartender, for a whiskey.
"I don't know, Garvin, you sure have run-up a big bill in here." The bartender told him.
" I know," Garvin replied, "But I'm flat broke, and I sure

could use a drink."

"OK," The barkeep told him, "I'll just write your tab down on the piece of paper and pin it up here by the coat rack."

"Oh no, don't do that, I don't want everyone in town to see it.

"Don't worry," The bartender replied, "I'm going to cover it up with your parka until its paid!"

Why did the man refuse to eat the the rock samples of Fluorapatite, Chlorapatite, and Hydroxylapatite?
He didn't have much of an Apatite.

Why was the Stripper at the Geologist's Stag Party called "spathic"?
Because she had really good "cleavage".

Why did the biker carry a large piece of an extrusive, pyroclastic, igneous rock composed chiefly of volcanic ash as on his motorcycle?
He wanted to act tuff.

Geologists may seem picky, girls, but love's just a stone's pro away!

"It's no one's fault the earth shook," Tom quaked after the shock diminished.

If male geologists are saying "No more Mr. Gneiss Guy", female geologists are "Sugar and spice and everything gneiss."

Oceanography Jokes

A marine biologist developed a race of genetically engineered dolphins that could live forever if they were fed a steady diet of seagulls. One day his supply of the birds ran out, so he had to go out and trap some more. On the way back, he spied two lions asleep on the road. Afraid to wake them, he gingerly stepped over them. Immediately, he was arrested and charged with transporting gulls across sedate lions for immortal porpoises.

Oceanographers do it on the waves.
Oceanographers do it on the sea.
Oceanographers do it with currents.
Old oceanographers never die, they just stop having a whale of a time.
Old oceanographers never die, they just forget about any upswellings.
Old oceanographers never die, their tides just go into permanent wane.
Old oceanographers never die - they just stop making waves.

How is a dog and a marine biologist alike?
One wags a tail and the other tags a whale.

What do you call a FISH with no Eyes?
A FSH.

Dan had been studying whales for over 20 years and had made some thrilling breakthroughs regarding their communication. He had managed to decode many of their underwater sounds and to translate them into English. His latest research had proved that they can communicate over a distance of 300 miles. When asked what could they possibly have to say at such distances he replied, "As best as we can figure, it is something like - Hey, can you hear me now?"

A man walks into a bar with an octopus and says, "Fifty bucks says this octopus can play any musical instrument." The first challenger steps forward with a guitar. The octopus studies it for a minute then plays a riff that would stop Hendrix in his tracks.

The next guy hands over a trumpet. Again a quick examination followed by a tune Louis Armstrong would envy.

Finally a guy strolls up to the octopus with a bagpipe. The octopus looks at it completely perplexed. Sensing he's about to lose $50, the octopus' buddy pleads, "Can't you play this thing?"

"Play it?" the octopus replies. "If I can get its pajamas off, I'm gonna screw it."

Paleontology Jokes

A famous paleontologist was on his way to yet another lecture when his chauffeur offered an idea. "Hey, boss, I've heard your speech so many times I bet I could deliver it and give you the night off."

"Sounds great," the scientist said.

When they got to the auditorium, the paleontologist put on the chauffeur's hat and settled into the back row. The chauffeur walked to the lectern and delivered the speech. Afterward he asked if there were any questions.

"Yes," said one professor. Then he launched into a highly technical question.

The chauffeur was panic stricken for a moment but quickly recovered. That's an easy one, "he replied. "So easy, I' m going to let my chauffeur answer it!"

Paleontologists in India recently uncovered a new dinosaur. It's actually many dinosaurs but one is in the middle of all the others. The one in the middle is believed to have killed the others with a single roundhouse kick to the face.

The paleontologists wanted to call it ChuckNorrisaurs but the Indian government changed the name to Himotosaurous because it's simply not possible for Mr. Norris to be killed.

Have do you call a tyrannosaurus that is afraid of his own shadow ?
A nervous Rex.

Thesaurus: ancient reptile with an excellent vocabulary.

A fossil is an extinct animal. The older it is, the more extinct it is.

A paleonotology student writes home:

Dear Dad,
$chool i$ really great. I am making lot$ of friend$ and

$tudying very hard. With all my $tuff, I $imply can't think of anything I need, $o if you would like, you can ju$t $end me a card, a$ I would love to hear from you.
Love, Your $on.

The Reply:

Dear Son,
I kNOw that paleontology, ecoNOmics, and oceaNOgraphy are eNOugh to keep even an hoNOurs student busy. Do NOt forget that the pursuit of kNOwledge is a NOble task, and you can never study eNOugh.
Love, Dad

Four paleontology students were studying at Oxford they had done pretty well on all of the midterm exams. These four were so confident that the weekend before finals they decided to go up to London and party with some friends up there. So they did this and had a great time. However, with their hangovers and everything, they overslept all day Sunday and didn't make it back until early Monday morning. Rather than taking the final exam then, they found the professor and explained to him why they missed the final. They told him that they went up to London for the weekend, and had planned to come back in time to study, but that they had a flat tire on the way back, didn't have a spare and couldn't get help for a long time. The professor thought this over and then agreed that they could make up the final on the following day. The four were elated and relieved.
So, they studied that night and went in the next day at the time that the professor had told them. He placed them in separate rooms and handed each of them a test booklet and told them to begin.

They looked at the first problem, which was something simple about fossil preservation and was worth 5 marks. 'Great, 'they thought, 'this is going to be easy.'
They completed that problem and then turned the page.

They were unprepared, however, for what they saw on the next page. It said: For 95 marks: "Which tire was flat?"

What comes after extinction?
y-tinction, of course!
What comes after Y-tinction?
Z-end!

What kind of dinosaur can you ride in a rodeo?
A Bronco-saurus!

A professor stood before his class of 20 senior paleontology students, about to hand out the final exam. "I want to say that it's been a pleasure teaching you this semester. I know you've all worked extremely hard and many of you are off to grad school after summer break. So that no one gets their GP messed up because they might have been celebrating a bit too much this week, anyone who would like to opt out of the final exam today will receive a "B" for the course."
There was much rejoicing amongst the class as students got up, passed by the professor to thank him and sign out on his offer. As the last taker left the room, the professor looked out over the handful of remaining students and asked, "Any one else? This is your last chance." One final student rose up and took the offer. The professor closed the door and took attendance of those students remaining. "I'm glad to see you believe in yourself," he said. "You all have "A's."

Why are there old dinosaur bones in the museum?
Because they can't afford new ones!

Why did the Apatosaurus devour the factory?
Because she was a plant eater!

Why didn't the T-rex skeleton attack the museum visitors?
Because she had no guts!

Why did the dinosaur cross the road?
The chicken hadn't evolved yet!

Why do Tyrannosaurus like to eat snowmen?
Because they melt in their mouths.

Why did the Archaeopteryx catch the worm?
Because it was an early bird!

What do you call a fossil that doesn't ever want to work?
Lazy bones!

Mother: Why are you crying?
Daughter: Because I wanted to get a dinosaur for my baby brother .
Mother: That's no reason to cry.
Daughter: Yes it is! No one would trade me!

What dinosaur loves pancakes?
Tri-syrup-tops.

What did the female dinosaur call her blouse making business?
Try Sara's Tops.

How do dinosaurs pass exams?
With extinction!

What's the difference between dinosaurs and dragons?
Dinosaurs are still too young to smoke.

How do you clone a dinosaur?
Use a Photocopysaurus.

There once was a Caveman whose given name was "Onestone", so named because he had only one testicle. He hated that name and asked everyone not to call him Onestone!

After years and years of torment, Onestone finally cracked and said, "If anyone calls me Onestone again I will kill them!" The word got around and nobody called him that any more. Then one day a young woman named Blue Bird forgot and said, "Good morning, Onestone..."

He jumped up, grabbed her and took her deep into the forest where he made love to her all day and all night. He made love to her all the next day, until Blue Bird died from exhaustion. The word got around that Onestone meant what he promised he would do.

Years went by and no one dared call him by his given name until a woman named Yellow Bird returned to the village after being away for many year.

Yellow Bird, who was Blue Bird's cousin, was overjoyed when she saw Onestone. She hugged him and said, "Good to see you Onestone."

Onestone grabbed her, took her deep into the forest, then he made love to her all day, made love to her all night, made love to her all the next day, made love to her all the next night but, try as he might Yellow Bird wouldn't die! What is the moral of this story?

And the moral is .....You can't kill two birds with one stone.

When the caveman heard about the joys of sex he became homo-erectous

What did the caveman give his wife on Valentine's Day? Ughs and kisses.

Which newspaper do paleontologists read? The prehistoric times!

The tech support problem dates back to long before the industrial revolution, when primitive tribesmen beat out a rhythm on drums to communicate:

This fire help. Me Groog
Me Lorto. Help. Fire not work.
You have flint and stone?
Ugh
You hit them together?
Ugh
What happen?
Fire not work
(sigh) Make spark?
No spark, no fire, me confused. Fire work yesterday.
sigh You change rock?
I change nothing
You sure?
Me make one change. Stone hot so me soak in stream so stone not burn Lorto hand. Small change, shouldn`t keep Lorto from make fire, right?

Why do cavemen drag women by the hair instead of ankles?
So they don't fill up with rocks!!!

What music do cavemen enjoy?
Rock music!

One caveman said to the other, 'What's that big thing with the long neck writing Jane Eyre?'
The other one said, 'That's Bronte-saurus.'

What's a caveman's favorite sandwich?
Club.

In some rocks you can find the fossil footprints of fishes.

Many dead animals in the past changed to fossils while others preferred to be oil.

Optimist: A paleontologist who opens his wallet and expects to find money.

Physics Jokes

Why did the chicken cross the Mobius strip? To get to the same side.

Why did the chicken cross the road? Issac Newton: Chickens at rest tend to stay at rest, chickens in motion tend to cross roads.

A neutron walks into a bar; he asks the bartender, "How much for a beer?"
The bartender looks at him, and says "For you, no charge."

Prof: Some people have proposed using Krypton gas in scintillator detectors.
Grad Student: Won't that scare away the superstrings?

Two fermions walk into a bar. One orders a drink. The other says "I'll have what he's having."

Why won't Heisenbergs' operators live in the suburbs
They don't commute.

What is a quantum particle?
The dreams that stuff is made of!

If a pizza has a radius 'z' and a depth 'a' that pizza's volume can be defined Pi*z*z*a.

5. The past, the present, and the future all walk into a bar at the same time. It was tense.

Hey baby, if I were a particle and you were a quantum potential, would you let me penetrate your classically forbidden regions?

Man walks into a bar and says to the bartender, "Give me ten times the number of drinks everybody in here is drinking."

And the bartender says, "Now that, my friend, is an order of magnitude."

Two atoms bump into each other. One says "I think I lost an electron!"
The other asks, "Are you sure?"
"I'm positive."

What do you call it when atomic scientists grab their rods and gather around the old watering hole?
Nuclear fishin'

What do you get if you have Avogadro's number of donkeys?
Answer: molasses

It is said that the "J", also know as the "psi particle", has zero charm ".
I'm sure that's not true when you get to know it.

Renee Descartes walks into a bar, the bartender says "sir can I get you a martini "Descartes says "I don't think..." and he disappears .

How did the universe get destroyed?
Some strings were null terminated.

Werner Heisenberg and Rene Descartes are sitting at the bar.
The bartender asks if they want another round.
Descartes says, "I think not" and POOF he vanishes.
The bartender turns to Heisenberg and says, "Oh my God, did you see that!?"
Heisenberg says, "I can't be certain."

What is a tachyon?
A sub-atomic particle devoid of good taste.

All the physicists are playing hide and seek. Einstein is the 'den' and stands against the wall with his eyes closed and counts till 100 to enable all the physicists to run and hide. At the count of 100 Einstein turns around and finds Newton standing there.

He screams, "Newton, you are out!"

Newton says, "No, I 'm not!"

Einstein says, "Yes, you are. I can see you here in front of me".

Newton says, "I'm not out. Pascal is."

Einstein is a bit confused and starts to scratch his head and beard.

Newton says "Here, Let me explain"

He draws a square one meter by one meter on the floor and stands in the middle of it and says, "Newton per meter square is a Pascal, so it's Pascal who's out not me"

What do you call a nun who's had a sex change?
A Trans-sister

What do you get when you cross a snake with a Physicist?
A Bohr Constrictor.

What did the thermometer say to the graduated cylinder?
"You may have graduated but I've got many degrees"

When a snail crossed the road, he was run over by a turtle. Regaining consciousness in the emergency room, he was asked what caused the accident. "I really can't remember," the snail replied. "You see, it all happened so fast."

Enrico Fermi, while studying in college, was bored by his math classes. He walked up to the professor and said, "My classes are too easy!"

The professor looked at him, and said, "Well, I'm sure you'll find this interesting."

Then the professor copied 9 problems from a book to a paper and gave the paper to Fermi. A month later, the professor ran into Fermi, "So how are you doing with the problems I gave you?"

"Oh, they are very hard. I only managed to solve 6 of them."

The professor was visibly shocked, "What! But those are unsolved problems!"

Physics is not a religion.
If it were, we'd have a much easier time raising money.

A physical chemist is a student who goes to university thinking he might want to be a physicist, but gets intimated by the math.

Where does bad light end up?
Answer: In a prism!

A physics professor at a state university in Michigan was famous for his animated lectures. He was short and thin with wild white hair and an excited expression. In lecture he would through himself from the top of desks and throw frisbees to students in the back row to illustrate various principles.
One day in class he was spinning on an office chair holding weights in each hand when he lost his balance and tumbled into the first row.
He apologized to his class for going off on a tangent.

Does light have mass?
Of course not. It's not even Catholic!

You have the right to remain stationary

Time flies like an arrow.
Fruit flies like a banana.

Protons are positive.
Electrons are negative
Neutrons don't give a rat's ass.

Where is the center of the unverse?
Right in front of the quarterback of the universe.

Why did Schroedinger love poker?
He got to feed the kitty.

Radiation is when you smell manure.
Contamination is when you step in it.

I'm working to unify relativity and quantum mechanics into a single theory of everything. So far I've discovered beer is good.

There are two types of scientific facts.
Those that agree with your position and those that are very hard to interpret

A guy goes up to the librarian and asks, "I'd like a book on time travel."
"Didn't you return that last week?"

A guy goes up to librarian and says, "I'd like a book on probability."
"It might be on that shelf over there."

What is a physicist's favorite snack?
Quantum string cheese.

"I'm sorry we don't serve time travelers here," says the bartender. A time traveler walks into a bar.

My physics teacher said I had great potential. Then he pushed me out the window.

My physics teacher said my understanding of forces is the worst he's ever seen. I think he's pushing my leg.

They're wrong. Alcohol is a solution.

Angular momentum makes the world go 'round.

"That's all very well in practice, but will it work in theory?"

Why did the physicist go to the beach?
 To surf the quantum waves.

May the M x A be with you.

Photons don't matter.
Electrons don't matter
Positrons are another matter altogether.

If it doesn't matter, dies it anti matter?

Let's change the universe to fit the equations.

Then there was the absent minded physics professor who
kissed the bus goodbye and went to town on his wife.

Matter can be neither created nor destroyed. Nor can it be
returned without a receipt.

Of course time travel is possible.
 I told you that next week.

Physics: the most fun you can have with your clothes on.

The universe is a figment of it's own imagination.

I'm reading a book on anti gravity.
 I just can't seem to put it down.

Quarks aren't the only thing strange around here.

The real world is just a special case of the theoretical.

If a research project is not worth doing, it not worth doing
well.

String theory is like an erection.
The more you think about it the harder it gets.

Tombstone: Here Lies Heisenberg. Maybe.

Date a physicist. Get a big bang.

Matter comes in three states.
Matter that is broken.
Matter that doesn't work.
Matter that can't be found.

Why did the physicist need therapy?
He was having a meltdown.

Why did the physicist need therapy?
He had a few quarks.

What do photons drink?
Light beer.

If it isn't a matter of opinion is it an anti matter of opinion?

In God we trust. All others are sublet to peer review.

Tombstone: Here Lies Isaac Newton. A body at rest stays at rest.

Why did the particle physicist make his bed?
It was slepton.

Liberal arts majors have physics envy

If you eat pasta and anti pasta will you explode?

God does not play dice with the universe. He plays roulette.

When I was young we had to smash hydrogen and oxygen atoms together to make our own water.

When I was young physics was a kite and a key.

What did one photon say to the other photon?
I'm sick and tired of your interference.

A group of scientists were nominated for a Nobel prize. Using dental tools, they were able to sort out the smallest particles that mankind has yet discovered.
The group became known as " the Graders of the Flossed Quark."

Why did the two photons become a particle?
When they met they were getting bored with high speed Travel and decided to make something of themselves.

The cannibal cook was attaching his latest victim to the output of a 250KW short-wave transmitter. When queried about his cooking technique, he replied, "It makes them really crispy on the outside, but inside, they stay rare. It's the 'skin effect'."

I believe in the heat death of the Universe.
I'm a Kelvinist.

Heisenberg is out for a drive when he's stopped by a traffic cop. The cop says "Do you know how fast you were going?" Heisenberg says "No, but I know where I am."

Puns about nuclear physicists are particularly funny.

A small furry mammal walks into a bar and orders a drink. The bartender says, "Sorry, our occupancy is only $6.02*10^{20}$." We can't serve a mole."

The Stanford Linear Accelerator Center was known as SLAC, until the big earthquake, when it became known as SPLAC. SPLAC? Stanford Piecewise Linear Accelerator.

Q. Why is Epsilon afraid of Zeta?
A. Because Zeta Eta Theta.

Several physicists went to see a Broadway show a couple of weeks ago. After the show ended, everybody in the theater stood up and headed for the exit.
While we were waiting for the people in the seats next to us to exit therow, one commented that this was a "mass exodus."
Then another looked at him and asked, "Are you sure? How do you know it's mass and not weight?"
The first replied, "Because we're not being forced."

Q. What did one electron say to the other electron?
A. Don't get excited. You'll only get into a state!

Q. What do you call a Catholic service that is very very important?
A. Critical Mass

A Higgs-Boson particle goes into a church and the preacher says, "Higgs-Boson's aren't allowed in here. You call yourself the God particle; that's sacrilegious!
The Higgs-Boson particle says, "If you don't allow Higgs-Boson particles, how do you have mass?"

Heisenberg and Schrödinger are driving in a car and they get pulled over. The police officer asks, "Do you know how fast you were going?"
Heisenberg says, "Well, not really but I can tell you exactly where I was."
The officer thinks that this peculiar response is grounds for a search, and he finds a dead cat in the trunk, and he says, "Do you guys know that there's a dead cat in your trunk?"
And Schrödinger says, "Well, I do now!"

A student recognizes Einstein in a train and asks: Excuse me, professor, but does New York stop by this train?

"If you roll an orange across a table, what physical force brings it to a halt?
"Pulp Friction!"

Chuck Norris is the only human being to display the Heisenberg uncertainty principle -- you can never know both exactly where and how quickly he will roundhouse-kick you in the face.

Heisenberg dies and goes to Heaven
God tells him that now he is in Heaven, all things can be revealed.
Heisenberg says - "That's fine. Please O Lord explain to me why the fine structure constant is 1/137"
God says 'No problem', clicks His fingers and a blackboard and chalk appear. God begins to write equations. Heisenberg watches and comments
After equation 1: Ja, Ja, korrect. Das ist richtig.
After equation 2: Ja, korrect. Das ist richtig.
After equation 3: Nein! Nein! Nein!. Das ist nicht korrect!

A 747 was flying along and was full of Polish people. As they were going past some beautiful landmarks, the pilot came over the intercom and instructed all who were interested in seeing the landmark to look out the right side of the plane. Many passengers did so, and the plane promptly crashed. Why?
Too many poles in the right hand plane.

Three Graduates are peeing in a bathroom.
The UGA graduate finishes, goes over and washes his hands very well using lots of soap and water, and says "at UGA, they teach us to be clean".
The Clemson graduate finishes peeing, and washes his hands with a very small amount of soap and water and says "at Clemson they teach us how conserve resources".
The Georgia Tech graduate finishes and walks right towards the door. On his way out he says "At Tech they teach us not to piss on our hands".

A photon checks into a hotel.
"May I take your bags?" asks the bellhop.
"No. I'm traveling light"

A quantum particle comes to a fork in the road and takes both of them.

A string walks into a bar with a few friends and orders a beer. The bartender says, "I'm sorry, but we don't serve strings here." The string walks away a little upset and sits down with his friends. A few minutes later he goes back to the bar and orders a beer. The bartender, looking a little exasperated, says, "I'm sorry, we don't serve strings here." So the string goes back to his table. Then he gets an idea. He ties himself in a loop and messes up the top of his hair. Then he walks back up to the bar and orders a beer. The bartender squints at him and says, "Hey, aren't you a string?"
And the string says, "Nope, I'm a frayed knot."

What do string theorists use to preserve their modesty?
G-strings.

What happens when two string theorists marry?
10^{500} children across the multiverse, but all with differing amounts of dark energy.

What do you get when string theorists party?
Entanglement.

What do you get when you give a string theorist plenty of rope?
 A Gordian Knot.

What happens when two string theorists have an argument?
Branes collide.

What's the difference between a good string theorist and a bad one?

The good one predicts nothing; the bad one predicts everything!

What do undead string theorists absolutely crave?
Branes.

It is said that papers in string theory are published at a rate greater than the speed of light. This, however, is not problematic since no information is being transmitted.

How many string theorists does it take to play hide and seek?

$10^{500} + 1$ … so that there exists at least one universe with two people in it.

A tachyon walks into a bar. The bartender says, "Hey, we don't serve your kind, here!"
The tachyon says, "You did tomorrow."

Werner Heisenberg, Kurt Gödel and Noam Chomsky walk into a bar.
Heisenberg looks around the bar and says, "Because there are three of us and because this is a bar, it must be a joke. But the question remains, is it funny or not?"
Gödel thinks for a moment and says, "Well, because we're inside the joke, we can't tell whether it's funny or not. We'd have to be outside looking in."
Chomsky looks at both of them and says, "Of course, it's funny. You're just telling it wrong."

A young physicist, upon learning that he was denied tenure after six productive years at a University in San Francisco, requested a meeting with the Provost for an explanation, and a possible appeal.
At the meeting, the Provost told the young physicist, " I'm sorry to tell you that the needs of the University have shifted somewhat, during the past six-years leading up to your tenure decision. In point of fact, what we now require is a female, condensed-matter experimentalist. Unfortunately,

you are a male, high-energy theorist!"
Dejected but not defeated, the young physicist thought for a moment about the implications of the Provost's words. " Sir," he said, "I would be willing to convert in two of the three categories you mention, but ... I'll never agree to become an experimentalist!"

What do you call a resistance reliant electric stove built over a gas one?
Ohm on the range.

Researchers in Fairbanks Alaska announced last week that they have discovered a superconductor which will operate at room temperature.

What did the neutrino say to the Higgs boson?
Here's another fine mass you've gotten me into

Overheard after a student failed a physics test miserably:
Nuclear, Hydrogen, Atomic, My test- They can all be bombs.

A general working on the Manhattan project had great faith in Enrico Fermi's work, but it looked as if the other scientists' theory about splitting the atom and causing a chain reaction using uranium rather than thorium was gaining favor.
The general, despondent, thought that he would give Fermi one last chance. He wrote up a requisition for one more shipment of thorium and passed it on to his clerk. Just as he did so, he began to smile rather than pout.
His clerk asked, "Why the sudden change in mood, sir?"
The general replied, "That's because I just realized that I approved Fermi's last thorium."

One understands that the Catholic Church has lots of Mass, (and also acceleration, see the counter-reformation) and by Force=Mass * Acceleration, it is a big force in history. I think Protestantism has no mass, so it has no force, so why does people have the "Protestant work ethic?" It just does not make any sense!

Which USA cell phone carrier is banned from Geneva?
Cingularity.

The particle physicist was tired of his work - he'd been trying to discover the loveton (the hypothetical particle that carries the force of attraction between two people) and he was getting nowhere. 'What I need,' he said to himself, 'is a good long holiday doing something completely different. 'So he went to his travel agent and got some holiday brochures and looked through them, trying to decide what to do. Skiing in the Alps? No - too near CERN.
Scuba diving on the barrier reef? No - he'd forever be trying to calculate the pressure he was under at any particular depth.
At last, just as he was about to give up and go back to his collider, he spotted a small ad in the classified section that appeared to be just the thing. 'SAILING HOLIDAYS',
it declared. 'Come and be part of the crew of a sailing vessel. Get away from it all.'
Well, this looked like just the thing, so he picked up the phone and dialedthe number. A voice answered. 'Yes?'
'Uhmmm, well, I saw your advertisement, and I was wondering if I might book a place on one of your sailing holidays..?'
'Ah, well, you'd have to speak to the Captain of the ship about that. Hang on, and I'll get him for you.'
A long pause. Finally, a deep gruff voice came on. 'Captain Higgs speaking.
You want to go on the sailing trip?'
'Yes,' answered the physicist.
'Well, you're only just in time. We leave next week, and there's only two places left. Would you rather be the cook or the bo'sun?'
The physicist thought for a minute. 'I'd rather be the bo'sun, I think,' he said at last.
'Good.. ' replied the captain, and then went on to give details of where and when the ship was leaving. Next week, the physicist was sailing for foreign shores.

He had a wonderful time on the ship, and came back to his work refreshed and ready to go (though he never did discover the loveton). He never did forget
the trip, or the holiday he spent as Higg's Bo'sun.

If you broke the law of gravity, would you get a suspended sentence?

All power corrupts, but we need the electricity.

Question: What did the monk say when he got shocked?
Answer: Ohmmmmm

Sir Isaac Newton had a theory of how to get the best outcomes in a courtroom. He suggested to lawyers that they should drag their arguments into the late afternoon hours. The English judges of his day would never abandon their 4 o'clock tea time, and therefore would always bring down their hammer and enter a hasty, positive decision so they could retire to their chambers for a cup of Earl Grey.
This tactic used by the British lawyers is still recalled as Newton's Law of Gavel Tea.

Why do all the other subatomic particles have a love/hate relationship with the quarks? Because they are both strange and charming at the same time.

How does one welcome a high-ranking particle which forms totally-symmetric composite quantum states, onto a ship?
One pipes it on board with a Boson's Whistle.

What is the subatomic particle babe?
A gravitron, because she is so attractive.

Atomic cows tend to muon.

I caught my daughter playing with the electrical outlet, and she gave herself quite a shock. I had to ground her.

I have a quantum car. Every time I look at the speedometer I get lost...

The answer to the problem was "log(1+x)". A student copied the answer from the good student next to him, but didn't want to make it obvious that he was cheating, so he changed the answer slightly, to "timber(1+x)"

Physics professor has been doing an experiment, and has worked out an empirical equation that seems to explain his data. He asks the math professor to look at it. A week later, the math professor says the equation is invalid. By then, the physics professor has used his equation to predict the results of further experiments, and he is getting excellent results, so he asks the math professor to look again. Another week goes by, and they meet once more. The math professor tells the physics professor the equation does work, " But only in the trivial case where the numbers are real and positive."

Profesor Miller's colleague, Professor Gonnen Dunnit of the physics department, has spent a lifetime pursuing the as-of-yet unreachable goal of creating cold fusion in the lab. In his latest effort, he used molecules from vegetables to trigger the process on the atomic level.
During one attempt, it seemed that Professor Dunnit actually achieved his goal - the process resulted in a spherical burst of energy. The professor wrote it up and submitted it, but no other scientist could duplicate his results. The Nobel Prize committee considered his results but dismissed Professor Dunnit's efforts, saying he had only created a ball of corn fusion.

If you do research in optics, you will have to do some light reading.

One day in class, Richard Feynman was talking about angular momentum. He described rotation matrices and mentioned that they did not commute. He said that Sir William Hamilton discovered noncommutivity one night when he was taking a walk in his garden with Lady Hamilton. As they sat down on a bench, there was a moment of passion. It was then that he discovered that AB did not equal BA.

What do you call a green fractionally charged particle with a half life of 130 million years?
Jurassic Quark.

If sound does not travel in a vacuum why is a vacuum so noisy?

Question: Why do soccer club Fermi and club Bose never play a match against each other?
Answer: They can't agree about the spin of the ball.

Why did the chicken cross the road?
Albert Einstein: Whether the chicken crossed the road or the road crossed the chicken depends on your frame of reference.

A hydrogen atom came running into a police station asking for help....
Hydrogen atom: Someone just stole my electron!!
Policeman: Are you sure?
Hydrogen atom: Yes, I'm positive
Policeman: Oh, I thought you were just being negative again.

"Do you have any books on electricity?"
"Watt we have is not current, but might shed some light on the subject. Wire you asking?"

The experimentalist comes running excitedly into the theorist's office, waving a graph taken off his latest experiment. "Hmmm," says the theorist, "That's exactly where you'd expect to see that peak. Here's the reason (long logical explanation follows)."
In the middle of it, the experimentalist says "Wait a minute", studies the chart for a second, and says, "Oops, this is upside down." He fixes it.

"Hmmm," says the theorist, "you'd expect to see a dip in exactly that position. Here's the reason...".

Couples should torque in order to resolve their differences.

What is uttered by a sick duck?
Quark!

When Archimedes got up out of the bath and noticed how much water had
spilled out of the tub, he said, "I've got to get out of displace!"

What do you call the random path that a cow makes as it grazes in the pasture?
Bovinian motion.

Ohm's Law was good enough in its time, but that time is past. It is a rankly discriminatory piece of legislation and should be repealed or severely amended. Current should be directly proportional to both voltage and resistance, or inversely proportional to both, or proportional to neither.

A Princeton plasma physicist is at the beach when he discovers an ancient looking oil lantern sticking out of the sand. He rubs the sand off with a towel and a genie pops out. The genie offers to grant him one wish. The physicist retrieves a map of the world from his car an circles the Middle East and tells the genie, "I wish you to bring peace in this region".
After 10 long minutes of deliberation, the genie replies, "Gee, there are lots of problems there with Lebanon, Iraq, Israel, and all those other places. This is awfully embarrassing. I've never had to do this before, but I'm just going to have to ask you for another wish. This one is just too much for me".
Taken aback, the physicist thinks a bit and asks, "I wish that the Princeton tokamak would achieve scientific fusion energy break-even."
After another deliberation the genie asks, "Could I see that map again?"

Albert Einstein married his cousin. He had tried to date outside his family circle, but he never found any women appealing - especially in the boob department - that weren't within his familial group. He postulated that there is a special attraction to women in one's own family in his Theory of Relative Titty.

Anything that doesn't matter has no mass.

What do physicist enjoy doing the most at baseball games? The 'wave'.

What is the difference between a physicist, an engineer, and a mathematician?
If an engineer walks into a room and sees a fire in the middle and a bucket of water in the corner, he takes the bucket of water and pours it on the fire and puts it out.
If a physicist walks into a room and sees a fire in the middle and a bucket of water in the corner, he takes the bucket of water and pours it eloquently around the fire and lets the fire put itself out.
If a mathematician walks into a room and sees a fire in the middle and a bucket of water in the corner, he convinces himself there is a solution and leaves.

A high school physics teacher had a summer job as a beach lifeguard. He noted that the best tanned babes flirted the most throughout the summer, though they never found steady boyfriends. He theorized that: A body in lotion trends to stray emotion.

Gravity brings me down

Neutrinos have bad breadth.

Gravity is a law. Lawbreakers will be brought down!

In a certain debating society, the subject of relativity came up. One member took it upon himself to elucidate the all-absorbing scientific theory. He explained, propounded and examined the subject for an hour. When he had finished, from sheer exhaustion, a listener spoke up.

'You know, after listening to you, I think you are really greater than Einstein himself. According to statistics, only twelve men in the whole world understand Einstein — but nobody understands you."

Albert Einstein had been working on his theory of relativity a lot and he was just about finished. He was almost ready to publish his work. However, he was under a lot of stress so he thought he would go on vacation to Mexico.

Albert had a glorious two week vacation and was having the time of his life. On the last night he was staying there he decided to take a walk along the beach and watch the sunset. As he watched the sun go down he thought of the light of the sun and then the speed of light. You see, he had been using the speed of light in a lot of his calculations but he didn't decide on what symbol to use for it. Greek had been so overused.

Just at that moment Senior Wensez was also walking along the beach in the opposite direction. Albert caught him out of the corner of his eye and remarked suddenly, "Do you not zink zat zee speed of light is very fast?"

Senior Wensez paused for a moment and replied, "Si."

An experimental physicist performs an experiment involving two cats, and an inclined tin roof. The two cats are very nearly identical; same sex, age, weight, breed, eye and hair color. The physicist places both cats on the roof at the same height and lets them both go at the same time. One of the cats fall off the roof first so obviously there is some difference between the two cats.

What is the difference? One cat has a greater mew.

Polymer physicists are into chains.

French physicist Ampere (1775-1836) had two cats, one big and a one small, and he loved them very much. But when the door was closed cats couldn't enter or exit the room. So Ampere ordered two holes to be made in his door: one big for the big cat, and one small for the small cat.

A psychologist makes an experiment with a mathematician and a physicist. He puts a good-looking, naked woman in a bed in one corner of the room and the mathematician on a chair in another one, and tells him: "I'll halve the distance between you and the woman every five minutes, and you're not allowed to stand up."
The mathematician runs away, yelling: "In that case, I'll never get to this woman!".
After that, the psychologist takes the physicist and tells him the plan. The physicist starts grinning. The psychologist asks him: "But you'll never get to this woman?"
The physicists tells him: "Sure, but for all practical things this is a good approximation."

There is this farmer who is having problems with his chickens. All of the sudden, they are all getting very sick and he doesn't know what is wrong with them. After trying all conventional means, he calls a biologist, a chemist, and a physicist to see if they can figure out what is wrong. So the biologist looks at the chickens, examines them a bit, and says he has no clue what could be wrong with them. Then the chemist takes some tests and makes some measurements, but he can't come to any conclusions either. So the physicist tries. He stands there and looks at the chickens for a long time without touching them or anything. Then all of the sudden he starts scribbling away in a notebook. Finally, after several gruesome calculations, he exclaims, "I've got it! But it only works for spherical chickens in a vacuum."

186,000 miles per second. It's not just a good idea, it's the law.

Two electron convicts are sitting in a jail cell together.
The first one says, "What are you in for?"
The second one says, "For attempting a forbidden transition."

Why did the chicken cross the Mobius strip?
To get to the same side.

Why did the chicken cross the road?
Issac Newton: Chickens at rest tend to stay at rest, chickens in motion tend to cross roads.

Why did the chicken cross the road?
Albert Einstein: Whether the chicken crossed the road or the road crossed the chicken depends on your frame of reference.

What element was discovered by politicians?
Balonium.

Gravity brings me down.

Neutrinos have bad breadth.

If it's green and wiggles, it's biology.
If it stinks, it's chemistry.
If it doesn't work, it's physics.

WATT is the unit of power?

Did you hear about the guy who wanted his windows cleaned?
He had Bose-Einstien condensation.

Stone walls do not a prism make, nor iron bars a diffraction grating.

What is the difference between a Quantum Theorist and a Beauty Therapist?

The Quantum Theorist uses Planck's Constant as a foundation, whereas the Beauty Therapist uses Max Factor.

What's the difference between Max Factor and Quantum Theorist?
Max Factor has models that work.
A young fellow was in the hospital having a brain scan. The doctor returned and told him he had good news and bad news. 'The bad news is that you have a brain disease and will probably die. The good news is that this hospital has developed a procedure for brain transplants and you qualify. Even better, there has been a wreck just outside the hospital doors and we have two fresh brains waiting for a transplant. You are lucky as both brains came from well educated men, in fact one was a political science major and the other from a physicist."
The doctor explained further that the polysci's brain costs $250,000 while the physicist's brain costs $19.95.
A little puzzled, the patient asked why the physicist's brain was so much cheaper.
The doctor replied, "Because it's been used ! "

Professor Niels Bohr, a famous Applied Mathematician-Physicist, had a horse shoe over his desk. One day a student asked if he really believed that a horse shoe brought luck. Professor Bohr replied, "I understand that it brings you luck if you believe in it or not."

One student in Rutherford's lab was very hard-working. Rutherford had noticed it and asked one evening: "Do you work in the mornings too?"
"Yes," proudly answered the student sure he would be commended.
"But when do you think?" amazed Rutherford.

When Gladstone met Michael Faraday, he asked him whether his work on electricity would be of any use.

"Yes, sir" remarked Faraday with prescience, "One day you will tax it."

During a lecture, professor Dirac made a mistake in an equation he was writing on the blackboard. A courageous student raises his finger and says timidly : "Professor Dirac, I do not understand equation 2." Dirac continues writing without any reaction. The student supposes Dirac has not heard him and raises his finger again, and says, louder this time: "Professor Dirac, I do not understand equation 2." No reaction. Somebody on the first row decides to intervene and says: "Professor Dirac, that man is asking a question."
"Oh," Dirac replies, I thought he was making a statement."

A sign hanging on a laboratory door: "Gone Nuclear Fission."

What's a nuclear physicist's favorite meal? Fission chips.

A quantum physicist walks into a bar... ...maybe.

What's the difference between a quantum mechanic and an auto mechanic?
 The quantum mechanic can get inside without opening the door.

Who solves mysteries involving electricity? Sherlock Ohms

Why is electricity so dangerous? Because it doesn't know how to conduct itself properly.

The law of gravity says no fair jumping up without coming back down.

When they broke open molecules, they found they were only stuffed with atoms. But when they broke open atoms, they found them stuffed with explosions.

A vibration is a motion that cannot make up its mind which way it wants to go.

There is a tremendous weight pushing down on the center of the Earth because of so much population stomping around up there these days.

The Top Ten Lies Told by Graduate Students

10. It doesn't bother me at all that my college roommate is making $80,000 a year on Wall Street.

9. I'd be delighted to proofread your book/chapter/article.

8. My work has a lot of practical importance.

7. I would never date an undergraduate.

6. Your latest article was so inspiring.

5. I turned down a lot of great job offers to come here.

4. I just have one more book to read and then I'll start writing.

3. The department is giving me so much support.

2. My job prospects look really good.

1. No really, I'll be out of here in only two more years.

Top Five Lies Told By Teaching Assistants:

5. I'm not going to grant any extensions.

4. Call me any time. I'm always available.

3. It doesn't matter what I think; write what you believe.

2. Think of the midterm as a diagnostic tool.

1. My other section is much better prepared than you guys.

You just might be a graduate student if...

...you can analyze the significance of appliances you cannot operate.
...your office is better decorated than your apartment.
...you have ever, as a folklore project, attempted to track the progress of your own joke across the Internet.
...you are startled to meet people who neither need nor want to read.
...you have ever brought a scholarly article to a bar.
...you rate coffee shops by the availability of outlets for your laptop.
...everything reminds you of something in your discipline.
...you have ever discussed academic matters at a sporting event.
...you have ever spent more than $50 on photocopying while researching a single paper.
...there is a microfilm reader in the library that you consider "yours."
...you actually have a preference between microfilm and microfiche.
...you can tell the time of day by looking at the traffic flow at the library.
...you look forward to summers because you're more

productive without the distraction of classes.

...you regard ibuprofen as a vitamin.

...you consider all papers to be works in progress.

...professors don't really care when you turn in work anymore.

...you find the bibliographies of books more interesting than the actual text.

...you have given up trying to keep your books organized and are now just trying to keep them all in the same general area.

...you have accepted guilt as an inherent feature of relaxation.

...you find yourself explaining to children that you are in "20th grade".

...you start refering to stories like "Snow White et al."

...you often wonder how long you can live on pasta without getting scurvy.

...you look forward to taking some time off to do laundry.

...you have more photocopy cards than credit cards.

...you wonder if APA style allows you to cite talking to yourself as "personal communication."

Laws of Funny Feline Physics

Law of Cat Inerti: A cat at rest will tend to remain at rest, unless acted upon by some outside force - such as the opening of cat food, or a nearby scurrying mouse.

Law of Cat Motion: A cat will move in a straight line, unless there is a really good reason to change direction.

Law of Cat Magnetism: All blue blazers and black sweaters attract cat hair in direct proportion to the darkness of the fabric.

Law of Cat Thermodynamics: Heat flows from a warmer to a cooler body, except in case of a cat, in which case all heat flows to the cat.

Law of Cat Stretching: A cat will stretch to a distance proportional to the length of the nap just taken.

Law of Cat Sleeping: All cats must sleep with people whenever possible, in a position as uncomfortable for the people involved, and as comfortable for the cat, as possible.

Law of Cat Elongation: A cat can make her body long enough to reach any counter top that has anything remotely interesting on it.

Law of Cat Obstruction: A cat must lie on the floor in a position to obstruct the maximum amount of human foot traffic.

Law of Cat Acceleration: A cat will accelerate at a constant rate, until he gets good and ready to stop.

In May a few years ago, the "Momentum, Heat and Mass Transfer " exam paper contained the question: "Is Hell exothermic or endothermic? Support your answer with proof."
Most students wrote proofs of their beliefs using Boyle's Law or similar. One student, however, wrote the following:
First, we must postulate that if souls exist, they must have some mass. If they do, then a mole of souls also must have a mass. So, at what rate are souls moving into hell and at what rate are souls leaving? I think we can safely assume that once a soul gets to Hell, it does not leave. Therefore, no souls are leaving.
As for souls entering Hell, let's look at the different religions that exist in the world today. Some religions say that if you are not a member of their religion, you will go to Hell. Since there are more than one of these religions, and people do not belong to more than one religion, we can project that all people and all souls go toHell. With the birth and death rates what they are, we can expect the number of souls in Hell to increase exponentially. Now, we look at the rate of change in

the volume of Hell. Boyle's Law states that in order for the temperature and pressure in Hell to stay the same, the ratio of the mass of the souls and volume needs to stay constant. [Answer 1] So, if Hell is expanding at a slower rate than the rate at which souls enter Hell, then the temperature in Hell will increase until all Hell breaks loose.

[Answer 2] Of course, if Hell is expanding at a rate faster than the increase in souls in Hell, then the temperature and pressure will drop until Hell freezes over.

So which is it? If we accept the postulate (given to me by Melody Song during freshman year) that "it'll be a cold day in Hell before I sleep with you", and taking into account that I still have not succeeded in having sexual relations with her, then [Answer 2] cannot be correct;

...... thus, Hell is exothermic.

The student got the only A.

Statistics Jokes

A somewhat advanced society has figured how to package basic knowledge in pill form. A student, needing some learning, goes to the pharmacy and asks what kind of knowledge pills are available. The pharmacist says "Here's a pill for English literature." The student takes the pill and swallows it and has new knowledge about English literature! "What else do you have?" asks the student.
"Well, I have pills for art history, biology, and world history," replies the pharmacist.
The student asks for these, and swallows them and has new knowledge about those subjects!
Then the student asks, "Do you have a pill for statistics?"
 The pharmacist says "Wait just a moment..." and goes back into the storeroom and brings back a whopper of a pill that is about twice the size of a jawbreaker and plunks it on the counter.
"I have to take that huge pill for statistics?" inquires the student.
The pharmacist understandingly nods his head and replies "Well, you know statistics always was a little hard to swallow."

Statistics: The discipline that proves the average person has one testicle.

Statistics are like a bikini - what they reveal is suggestive, but what they conceal is vital.

If there is a 50-50 chance that something can go wrong, then 9 times out of ten it will.

Statistics means never having to say you're certain.

Why did the statistician need therapy?
He had a non standard deviation.

Yes. I've probably heard the latest statistics joke.

Sign on statisticians office "Precision guesswork done here."

A famous statistician would never travel by airplane,
because he had studied air travel and estimated the
probability of there being a bomb on any given flight
was 1 in a million, and he was not prepared to accept
these odds. One day a colleague met him at
a conference far from home. "How did you get here,
by train?"
"No, I flew" "What about the possibility of a bomb?"
'Well, I began thinking that if the odds of one bomb are
1:million, then the odds of TWO bombs are
(1/1,000,000) x (1/1,000,000). This is a very, very small
probability, which I can accept. So, now I bring my
own bomb along!"

"Give us a copper, Guv" said the beggar to the
Treasury statistician, when he waylaid him in Parliament
square. "I haven't eaten for three days."
"Ah," said the statistician, "and how does that compare
with the same period last year?"

The larger the sample size (n) the more confident you can be
that your sample mean is a good representation of the
population mean.
In other words, the "n" justifies the means.

You know how dumb the average guy is?
Well, by definition, half of them are even dumber than that.

There was this statistics student who, when
driving his car, Would always accelerate hard before
coming to any junction, whizz straight over it , then
slow down again once he'd got over it.
One day, he took a passenger, who was understandably
unnerved by his driving style, and asked him why he

went so fast over junctions. The statistics student replied, "Well, statistically speaking, you are far more likely to have an accident at a junction, so I just make sure that I spend less time there."

A new government 10 year survey cost $3,000,000,000 revealed that 3/4 of the people in America make up 75% of the population.

In earlier times, they had no statistics, and so they had to fall back on lies.

Old statisticians never die, they just undergo a transformation.

There was a very old Peanuts cartoon in which Charlie Brown was addressing his baseball team at the end of the season. He recited numerous dismal statistics such as : Runs scored by us 12, by opponents 125. At the end of the speech he yells out: "And what are we going to do about it?" to which the team answers in unison: "Get a new statistician!"

What is the definition of a statistician?
Someone who doesn't have the personality to be an accountant.

Fate laughs at probabilities.

Statistics is the art of never having to say you're wrong.

Variance is what any two statisticians are at.

A Bayesian is one who, vaguely expecting a horse, and catching a glimpse of a donkey, strongly believes he has seen a mule.

Four statisticians who were caught in a boating shop tossing packages of canvas around.
It turned out they were just fore-casting sales.

Smoking is a leading cause of statistics.

Logic is a systematic method for getting the wrong conclusion with confidence.

Statistics is a systematic method for getting the wrong conclusion with 95% confidence.

Studies have shown that the leading cause of death is life.

Statistics is like a man, with a bit of manipulation you can get out of it what you want.

Statisticians know all of the standard deviations.

These two friends decide to go rabbit hunting with bow and arrows. They convince their friend, the statistician, to come along since he doesn't get out very much. The three wait patiently out in the woods for a rabbit to pass by. Suddenly, a rabbit bolts across a clearing some distance away and races toward a dense patch of trees. The first hunter whips out his bow, strings an arrow, and lets fly. "Darn," he cries, "The arrow was a foot short."
Just then the rabbit bolts across the clearing from the other side of the woods. The second hunter whips out his bow, strings an arrow, and lets fly. "Darn" complains the second hunter, "the arrow went a foot long."
The rabbit once more emerges from the woods and races across the clearing. The statistician starts to raise his bow and then lowers it with a contemplative expression. He takes out the stub of a pencil, finds a crumpled envelope in a pants

pocket, and quickly executes some calculations on the back of the envelope. The he looks up, smiling, as the rabbit disappears for the final time and waves the envelope in the direction of the other two hunters. "Look at this--if you take the mean distance that the arrows went, we got the rabbit!"

43% of all statistics are worthless.

How do you statistically test for differences among professional women tennis players?
Perform an analysis of cornered covariance, known as an ANACORNCOVA

The statistics professor's failing students found it difficult to live within his means.

PROOF THAT ALL ODD NUMBERS ARE PRIME:
Mathematician -- 3 is prime, 5 is prime, 7 is prime, the rest follows by induction.
Statistician -- 3 is prime, 5 is prime, 7 is prime, 9 is experimental error so throw it out, 11 is prime, 13 is prime, the rest follows by induction.

Computer Scientist -- 3 is prime, 5 is prime, 7 is prime, 9 is prime, ...

I always find that statistics are hard to swallow and impossible to digest. The only one I can ever remember is that if all the people who go to sleep in church were laid end to end they would be a lot more comfortable.

Did you hear about the Statistician that couldn't get laid?
He decided a simulation was good enough.

Statistician: A Mathematician broken down by age and sex.

Three professors (a physicist, a chemist, and a statistician) are called in to see their dean. Just as they arrive the dean is called out of his office, leaving the three professors there. The professors see with alarm that there is a fire in the wastebasket.

The physicist says, "I know what to do! We must cool down the materials until their temperature is lower than the ignition temperature and then the fire will go out."
The chemist says, "No! No! I know what to do! We must cut off the supply of oxygen so that the fire will go out due to lack of one of the reactants."
While the physicist and chemist debate what course to take, they both are alarmed to see the statistician running around the room starting other fires. They both scream, "What are you doing?"
To which the statistician replies, "Trying to get an adequate sample size."

I asked a statistician for her phone number... and she gave me an estimate.

She was only the statistician's daughter, but she knew all the standard deviations.

Three statisticians were out in a boat, hunting ducks. After waiting for a while they saw one. The first statistician shot a meter high.
The second statistician shot a meter low.
The third statistician said, "We got it!".

43% of people think a pie chart is found in a bakery.

Torture the data long enough and they will confess to anything.

What did the z distribution say to the t distribution?
You may look like me but you're not normal.

Did you hear the one about the statistician?
Probably....

All probabilities are 50% ... either something happens, or it doesn't!

Statisticians say mean things.

Patient: "Will I survive this risky operation?"
Surgeon: "Yes, I'm absolutely sure that you will survive the operation."
Patient: "How can you be so sure?"
Surgeon: "9 out of 10 patients die in this operation, and yesterday died my ninth patient."

It is proven that the celebration of birthdays is healthy. Statistics show that those people who celebrate the most birthdays become the oldest.

Ten percent of all car thieves are left-handed.
All polar bears are left-handed.
If your car is stolen, there's a 10 percent chance it was taken by a polar bear.

If I had only one day left to live, I would live it in my statistics class: it would seem so much longer.

Learning Statistics is like taking a Mediterranean cruise. You gain a new appreciation for the vastness of the world; You meet dozens of new characters, half of them with Greek names; and After 2 hours you feel utterly seasick.

I used to think correlation implied causation. Then I took a statistics class. Now I don't.: Sounds like the class helped. Well, maybe.

Statistics play an important role in genetics. For instance, statistics prove that numbers of offspring is an inherited trait. If your parent didn't have any kids, odds are you won't either.

All dogs are animals.
All cats are animals.
Therefore, all dogs are cats.

Incidentally, did you know that using non-linear regression in research is currently out of line.

If you choose an answer to this question at random, what is the chance you will be correct?
A) 25%
B) 50%
C) 60%
D) 25%
According to a recent survey, 33 of the people say they participate in surveys.

According to a recent survey, a number of people said they despise participating in surveys. Accurate figures are not yet available as several of the surveyors remain in intensive care and are not available for comment. A recent survey of their boss indicated that 100% of bosses have openings available for future surveyors.

Yo momma is so mean, she has no standard deviation!

Did you hear about the statistician who invented a device to measure the weight of trees?
It's referred to as the log scale.

Statistics in the hands of an engineer are like a lamppost to a drunk--they're used more for support than illumination.

What do you call 100 statisticians at a tea party?
A A Z-Party.

A stats major was completely hung over the day of his final exam. It was a True/False test, so he decided to flip a coin for the answers. The stats professor watched the student the

entire two hours as he was flipping the coin...writing the answer...flipping the coin...writing the answer. At the end of the two hours, everyone else had left the final except for the one student. The professor walks up to his desk and interrupts the student, saying: "Listen, I have seen that you did not study for this statistics test, you didn't even open the exam. If you are just flipping a coin for your answer, what is taking you so long?"
The student replies bitterly (as he is still flipping the coin): " Shhh! I am checking my answers!"

How many statisticians does it take to change a light bulb?
5–7, with p-value 0.01

Did you hear about the statistician who took the Dale Carnegie course?
He improved his confidence from .95 to .99.

The statistics on sanity are that one out of every four Americans isvsuffering from some form of mental illness. Think of your three best friends. If they're okay, then it's you.

A researcher tried jalapenos on a stomach ulcer patient, and the ulcer went away. The researcher published an article "Jalapenos Cure Stomach Ulcers." The next patient subjected to the same treatment died. The researcher published a follow-up article "More Detailed Study Reveals That Jalapenos Cure 50% Of Stomach Ulcers".

A total of 4000 cans are opened around the world every second.
Ten babies are conceived around the world every second. Each time you open a can, you stand a 1 in 400 chance of becoming pregnant.

Actual fact: A Norwegian professor of statistics bears the name of Just Gjessing.

Clem asks Abner, "Ain't statistics wonderful?"
"How so?" says Abner.
"Well, according to statistics, there's 42 million alligator eggs laid every year. Of those only about half get hatched. Of those that hatch, three-fourths of them get eaten by predators in the first 36 days. And of the rest, only 5 percent get to be a year old because of one thing or another. Ain't statistics wonderful?"
Abner asks, "What's so wonderful about statistics?"
"Why, if it wasn't for statistics, we'd be up to our asses in baby alligators!"

A statistician and a normal joe are sitting in an airport hall waiting for their flight to go. The joe has terrible flight panic.
"Hey, don't worry. It's just every 10,000th flight that crashes."
"1:10000? So much? Then it surely will be mine!"
"Well, there is an easy way out. Simply take the next plane. It's much more probable that you go from a crashing to a non-crashing plane than the other way round. So you are already at 1:10000 squared."

A statistician can have his head in an oven and his feet in ice, and he will say that on the average he feels fine.

A researcher asked an experienced statistician what procedure should be used to obtain the correlation between two normally distributed variables that were artificially dichotomized. Why did the researcher suddenly rush from the statistician's office and run straight to the pharmacy to buy a bottle of carbon tet cleaning fluid?
The statistician told him a TETRACHORIC SOLUTION was appropriate for his problem!

In God we trust. All others must bring data.

A statistician is an accountant without the charisma.

A musician drove his statistician friend to a symphony concert one evening in his brand new mid-sized Chevy. When they arrived at the hall, all the parking spots were taken except one in a remote, dark corner of the lot. The musician quickly maneuvered his mid-sized Chevy into the space and they jumped out and walked toward the hall. They had only taken about ten steps when the musician suddenly realized he had lost his car key. The statistician was unconcerned because he knew the key had to be within one standard deviation of the car. They both retraced their steps and began searching the shadowed ground close to the driver's door. After groping on his hands and knees for about a minute, the musician bounced to his feet and bolted several hundred yards toward a large street light near the back of the concert hall. He quickly got down on all fours and resumed his search in the brightly lit area. The statistician remained by the car dumbfounded knowing that the musician had absolutely zero probability of finding the key under the street light.

Finally, after fifteen minutes, the statistician's keen sense of logic got the best of him. He walked across the lot to the musician and asked, "Why in the world are you looking for your key under the street light? You lost it back in the far corner of the lot by your car!" The musician in his rumpled and stained suit slowly got to his feet and muttered angrily, "I KNOW, BUT THE LIGHT IS MUCH BETTER OVER HERE!!"

Did you hear about the statistician who was thrown in jail? He now has zero degrees of freedom.

5 out of every 4 people have problems with fractions.

Three men are in a hot-air balloon. Soon, they find themselves lost in a canyon somewhere. One of the three men says, "I've got an idea. We can call for help in this canyon and the echo will carry our voices far." So he leans over the basket and yells out, "Helllloooooo! Where are we?" (They hear the echo several times.)

Fifteen minutes pass. Then they hear this echoing voice: "Helllloooooo! You're lost!!" One of the men says, "That must have been a statistician." Puzzled, one of the other men asks, "Why do you say that?"
The reply: "For three reasons: 1) he took a long time to answer, 2) he was absolutely correct, and 3) his answer was absolutely useless."

A biologist, a statistician, a mathematician, and a computer scientist are on a photo-safari in Africa. They drive out into the savannah in their jeep, stop, and scour the horizon with their binoculars.   The biologist: "Look! There's a herd of zebras! And there, in the middle: a white zebra!
It's fantastic! There are white zebras! We'll be famous!"
The statistician: "It's not significant. We only know there's one white zebra."
The mathematician: "Actually, we know there exists a
 zebra which is white on one side."
The computer scientist: "Oh no! A special case!"

Fett's Law: Never replicate a successful experiment.

Statisticians must stay away from children's toys because they regress so easily.

Two statisticians were travelling in an airplane from LA to New York. About an hour into the flight, the pilot announced that they had lost an engine, but don't worry, there are three left. However, instead of 5 hours it would take 7 hours to get to New York. A little later, he announced that a second engine failed, and they still had two left, but it would take 10 hours to get to New York. Somewhat later, the pilot again came on the intercom and announced that a third engine had died. Never fear, he announced, because the plane could fly on a single engine. However, it would now take 18 hours to get to New York. At this point, one statistician turned to the other and said, "Gee, I hope we don't lose that last engine, or we'll be up here forever!"

80% of all statistics quoted to prove a point are made up on the spot.

Why is it that the more accuracy you demand from an interpolation function, the more expensive it becomes to compute?
  That's the Law of Spline Demand.

Did you know that 87.166253% of all statistics claim a precision of results that is not justified by the method employed?

According to recent surveys, 51% of the people are in the majority.

Did you know that the great majority of people have more than the average number of legs? [It's obvious really; amongst the 57 million people in Britain there are probably 5,000 people who have only got one leg.
Therefore the average number of legs is

$$\frac{(5000 * 1) + (56,995,000 * 2)}{57,000,000} = 1.9999123......$$

Since most people have 2 legs........

Figures won't lie, but liars can figure.

There are two kinds of statistics, the kind you look up, and the kind you make up.
Rex Stout

A single death is a tragedy, a million deaths is a statistic.
Joseph Stalin

Statistics show that we lose more fools on this day than on all other
days of the year put together. This proves, by the numbers left in
stock, that one Fourth of July per year is now inadequate, the
country has grown so.
Mark Twain

Facts are stubborn, but statistics are more pliable.
Mark Twain

"There are three kinds of lies: lies, damned lies, and
statistics."
Attributed by Mark Twain to Benjamin Disraeli.

Statistics show that of those who contract the habit of eating,
very few survive.
Wallace Irwin

It only takes one person to make a statistically insignificant
difference.

A statistician was reprimanding his son.
"If I've told you n times I've told you n + 1 times...."

I could prove God statistically.
George Gallup

Like other occult techniques of divination, the statistical
method has a private jargon deliberately contrived to
obscure its methods from
non-practitioners.
G. O. Ashley

The government is extremely fond of amassing great
quantities of statistics. These are raised to the nth degree, the
cube roots are extracted, and the results are arranged into
elaborate and impressive displays. What must be kept ever in

mind, however, is that in every case, the figures are first put down by a village watchman, and he puts down anything he damn well pleases.
Sir Josiah Stamp

Why is a physician held in much higher esteem than a statistician?
A physician makes an analysis of a complex illness whereas a statistician makes you ill with a complex analysis

It only takes one person to make a statistically insignificant difference.

A statistician was reprimanding his son.
"If I've told you n times I've told you n + 1 times...."

In the computer industry, there are three kinds of lies:
Lies, damn lies, and benchmarks.

There are two kinds of people in this world.
Those who can extrapolate from incomplete data.

A Statistical Department is hiring mathematicians. Three recent graduates are invited for an interview: one has a degree in pure mathematics, another one in applied math, and the third one obtained his B.Sc. in statistics.
All three are asked the same question: "What is one third plus two thirds?"
The pure mathematician: "It's one."
The applied mathematician takes out his pocket calculator, punches in the numbers, and replies: "It's 0.999999999."
The statistician: "What do you want it to be?"

50% of the citizens of this country have a below average understanding of statistics.

A statistician is a person who draws a mathematically precise line from an unwarranted assumption to a foregone conclusion.

Statistical Analysis: Mysterious, sometimes bizarre, manipulations   performed upon the collected data of an experiment in order to obscure the fact that the results have no generalizable meaning for   humanity. Commonly, computers are used, lending an additional aura of unreality to the proceedings.

Did you hear about the politician who promised that, if he was elected, he'd make certain that _everybody_ would get an above average income?

`You haven't told me yet,'' said Lady Nuttal, ``what it is your fiance does for a living.''
``He's a statistician,'' replied Lamia, with an annoying sense of being on the defensive.
Lady Nuttal was obviously taken aback. It had not occurred to her that statisticians entered into normal social relationships.
The species, she would have surmised, was perpetuated in some collateral manner, like mules.
``But Aunt Sara, it's a very interesting profession,'' said Lamia warmly.
``I don't doubt it,'' said her aunt, who obviously doubted it very much. ``To express anything important in mere figures is so plainly impossible that there must be endless scope for well-paid advice on the how to do it. But don't you think that life with a statistician would be rather, shall we say, humdrum?''
Lamia was silent. She felt reluctant to discuss the surprising depth of emotional possibility which she had discovered below Edward's numerical veneer.
``It's not the figures themselves,'' she said finally. ``It's what you do with them that matters.''

Statisticians do it continuously but discretely.
Statisticians do it when it counts.
Statisticians do it with 95% confidence.
Statisticians do it with large numbers.
Statisticians do it with only a 5% chance of being rejected.
Statisticians do it with two-tail T tests.
Statisticians do it. After all, it's only normal.
Statisticians probably do it.
Statisticians do it with significance.
Probabilists do it on random walks.
Probabilists do it stochastically.
Statisticians do all the standard deviations.
Biostatisticians do it with power
Epidemiologists do it with populations
Bayesians do it with a posterior

Just try explaining the value of statistical summaries to the widow of the man who drowned crossing a stream with an average depth of four feet.

Why are statisticians misunderstood people
1. They speak only the Greek language.
2. They usually have long threatening names such as Bonferonni, Tchebycheff, Schatzoff, Hotelling, and Godambe. Where are the statisticians with names such as Smith, Brown, or Johnson?
3. They are fond of all snakes and typically own as a pet a large South American snake called an ANOCOVA.
4. . For perverse reasons, rather than view a matrix right side up they prefer to invert it.
5. . Rather than moonlighting by holding Amway parties they earn a few extra bucks by holding pocket-protector parties.
6. They are frequently seen in their back yards on clear nights gazing through powerful amateur telescopes looking for distant star constellations called ANOVA's.
7. They are 99% confident that sleep can not be induced in an introductory statistics class by lecturing on z-scores.

8. Their idea of a scenic and exotic trip is traveling three standard deviations above the mean in a normal distribution.
9. They manifest many psychological disorders because as young statisticians many of their statistical hypotheses were rejected.
10. They express a deaep-seated fear that society will someday construct tests that will enable everyone to make the same score. Without variation or individual differences the field of statistics has no real function and a statistician becomes a penniless ward of the state.

10% of the women had sex within the first hour of their first date.
20% of the men had sex in a non-traditional place.
36% of the women favor nudity.
45% of the women prefer dark men with blue eyes.
46% of the women experienced anal sex.
70% of the women prefer sex in the morning.
80% of the men have never experienced homosexual relations.
90% of the women would like to have sex in the forest.
99% of the women have never experienced sex in the office.
Conclusion: Statistically speaking, you have a better chance of having anal sex in the morning with a strange woman in the forest than to have sex in the office at the end of the day.
Moral: Do not stay late in the office. Nothing good will ever come of it!

The Ten Commandments of Statistical Inference

1. Thou shalt not hunt statistical inference with a shotgun.
2. Thou shalt not enter the valley of the methods of inference without an experimental design.
3. Thou shalt not make statistical inference in the absence of a model.
4. Thou shalt honor the assumptions of thy model.

5. Thy shalt not adulterate thy model to obtain significant results.
6. Thy shalt not covet thy colleagues' data.
7. Thy shalt not bear false witness against thy control group.
8. Thou shalt not worship the 0.05 significance level.
9. Thy shalt not apply large sample approximation in vain.
10. Thou shalt not infer causal relationships from statistical significance.

Mad Scientists

Did you hear about the mad scientist who married the Amish woman?
 He drove her buggy.
Did you hear about the mad scientist who worked for the woman peanut farmer?
 He made her nuts.

Did you hear about the mad scientist who trained the Olympic diver?
He sent him off the deep end.
Did you hear about the mad scientist who worked with the bungee jumper?
He pushed him over the edge.

Did you hear about the poor little baby who stayed with the mad scientist?
It went ga-ga.

Did you hear about the rocket experts who hired the mad scientist?
 They went ballistic
.

There was a mad scientist who kidnapped three colleagues, an engineer, a physicist, and a mathematician, and locked each of them in seperate cells with plenty of canned food and water but no can opener.
A month later, returning, the mad scientist went to the engineer's cell and found it long empty. The engineer had constructed a can opener from pocket trash, used aluminum shavings and dried sugar to make an explosive, and escaped. The physicist had worked out the angle necessary to knock the lids off the tin cans by throwing them against the wall. She was developing a good pitching arm and a new quantum theory.
The mathematician had stacked the unopened cans into a surprising solution to the kissing problem; his dessicated

corpse was propped calmly against a wall, and this was inscribed on the floor in blood:

Theorem: If I can't open these cans, I'll die.

Proof: assume the opposite...

Stephen Hawking Jokes

How does Stephen Hawking run?
On double A's.

What happens when Stephen Hawking dies?
The Windows Shutdown sound plays.

What did Stephen Hawking say when his computer crashed?
Nothing.

Stephen Hawking went on a date last night.
She left after 15 minutes complaining that she didn't like his tone.

When he dies, can you imagine Stephen Hawking in front of the stairway to heaven going: "Fuck..."

Stephen Hawking pressed F5 on his keyboard the other day.
He said he felt refreshed.

I'm Stephen Hawking, and I'm a PC.

What does Stephen Hawking do when he needs a shit?
Log out.

Stephen Hawking masturbating - Now there's a stroke of genius.

I've been trying to ring Stephen Hawking all week but he's never in.
All I ever get is an automated answer.

A thought. If I enter Stephen Hawking against his will, am I a rapist or a hacker?

Stephen Hawking can finally achieve an erection now that doctors have disabled his pop-up blocker.

After a few nights in the hospital Stephen Hawking is finally stable.
It only took 2 bricks behind his wheels.

Why do so many people, when discussing Stephen Hawking's recovery, use the phrase "He's looking forward..." He doesn't really have a choice.

Looks like Stephen Hawking's on his last wheels.

I think Stephen Hawking should have definitely renewed his subscription with Norton AntiVirus.

Steven Hawking was asked to address the annual dinner of the Dyslexic Association. So in order to be polite he switched off his spell-checker.

Limericks And Rhymes

An astronaut back from the stars.
Was bragging in all of the bars.
"You see this here penis
Won prizes on Venus
And took second place up on Mars."

From the public, his discovery brought cheers.
From his wife, it drew nothing but torrents of tears.
"For you see," said Ms. Halley,
"He used to come daily;
Now he comes once every 70 years!"

We cannot know where in the sky
A signal is lurking, or why.
We will search even though
The chances are low.
The payoff is well worth a try

There was once a cloner named Hector,
Who had problems in his private sector,
His wife was depressed,
'Cos his genes weren't expressed,
For lack of a functioning vector!

There was a lady. Miss Bright
Who could travel much faster than light.
She departed one day
In a relative way
And returned on the previous night.

To her friends, that Miss Bright use to chatter,
"I have learned something new about matter,
My speed was so great
That it increased my weight;
Yet I failed to become any fatter."

When Newton saw an apple fall, he found ...
a mode of proving that the earth turn'd round
in a most natural whirl, called gravitation;
and thus is the sole mortal who could grapple
since Adam, with a fall or with an apple

Her voice is so high it's absurd
It's so shrill that you can't hear a word
When she's something to say
She starts running away
So the pitch drops enough to be heard

There once was a man who said: 'Damn!
I can't possibly be in this tram
For how can I know
Both how fast that I go
And also the place where I am.'

There once was a girl named Irene,
Who lived on distilled kerosene.
But she started absorbin'
A new hydrocarbon,
And since then has never benzene!

A maiden at college, Miss Breeze,
Weighed down by B.A.s and Lit.D's,
Collapsed from the strain,
Said her doctor, "It's plain
You are killing yourself --- by degrees!"

A mathematician named Hall
Had a hexahedronical ball
The square of its weight
Times his pecker plus eight
Was two-thirds of three-fifths of fuck-all

There once was a chemist from Reed
Who never washed his hands before he peed.
The stuff on his hands
Got into his glans
And inhibited his ability to breed.

A Dozen, a Gross and a Score,
Plus three times the square root of four,
Divided by seven,
Plus five times eleven,
Equals nine squared and not a bit more.

A mosquito cried out in pain:
"A chemist has poisoned my brain!"
The cause of his sorrow
Was para-dichloro-
Diphenyltrichloroethane.

We cannot know where in the sky
A signal is lurking, or why.
We will search even though
The chances are low.
The payoff is well worth a try.

Archimedes, the well known truth-seeker,
Jumping out of his bath, cried "Eureka!
He ran half a mile
  Wearing only a smile,
And became the very first streaker.

There once was an old man of Esser,
Whose knowledge grew lesser and lesser,
It at last grew so small
He knew nothing at all
and now he's a college professor.

A certain phys ed referee
Considers all papers with glee:
"What's new is not true,
And what's true is not new,
Unless it was written by me."

There once was a fellow named Fisk
Whose fencing was exceedingly brisk.
So fast was his action
That by the Fitzgerald Contraction
His rapier soon was reduced to a disk.

A quantum mechanic's vacation
Had his colleagues in dire consternation.
For while studies had shown
That his speed was well known,
His position was pure speculation.

A biologist of world renown
Says a chromosome's gender is found
By being so bold
As to take a good hold
oOf it's genes...and then pull them down.

When studying bacterial mating
Lederberg found it frustrating
to make things look nice
and do everything twice
he invented replica plating

Bacteria have these flagella
That spin like a little propella.
They'll swim for a while
Up a river of bile
To your liver, which makes you turn yella.

Star light, star bright
First star I see tonight
I wish I may, I wish I might.
Aw crap
It's just a satellite.

There was a young fellow from Trinity,
Who took the square root of infinity.
But the number of digits,
 Gave him the fidgets;
He dropped Math and took up Divinity.

I had a brand new beaker once
Its gone beyond recall
For all the glass and pieces are
Embedded in the wall.

Little Willie was a chemist,
Little Willie is no more.
What he thought was H_2O,
Was H_2SO_4.

Willie saw some dynamite.
Couldn't understand it quite
Curiosity never pays.
It rained Willie seven days.

Little Willie from the mirror
Licked the mercury off.
Thinking in his childish error
It would cure his whooping cough.
At the funeral, Willie's mother
Smartly said to Mrs. Brown
"T'was a chilly day for Willie
When the mercury went down."

Mary had a kittle sheep
And with the sheep she went to sleep.
The sheep turned out to be a ram.
Mary had a little lamb.

Now I lay me down to study
I pray the Lord I won't go nutty
If I should fail to learn this junk
I pray the Lord I will not flunk
But if I do, don't pity me at all
Just lay my bones in the study hall
Tell my teacher I did my best
Then pile my books upon my chest
Now I lay me down to rest
If I should die before I wake
That's one less test I'll have to take

Mary had a little lamb,
Then two and three and four.
And each a perfect replica
of all that went before.
They followed her to school one day
Which was against the rule.
It made the children laugh and play
To see her flock at school.
The teacher turned the woolies out
To wait the bell at four.
But when the children tried to leave
More sheep had jammed the door.
"What makes those lambs love Mary so?"
The eager children fish.
Says teacher, dialing 9-1-1:
"She's got the Petri dish."

The microbe is so very small
You cannot make him out at all.
But many sanguine people hope
To see him down a microscope.
His jointed tongue that lies beneath
A hundred curious rows of teeth;
His seven tufted tail with lots
Of lovely pink and purple spots
On each of which a pattern stands,
Composed of forty separate bands;
His eyebrows of a tender green;
All these have never yet been seen
But Scientists, who ought to know,
Assure us they must be so ...
Oh! let us never, never doubt
What nobody is sure about!

The Grand old Duke of York,
He had ten thousand men,
He marched them up to the top of hill,
And he marched them down again.
When they were up they were up,
When they were down they were down.
When they were only half way up,
They were simultaneously up and down,
They were merely obeying the laws of quantum mechanics.

Hymn To Science

Science! thou fair effusive ray
From the great source of mental day,
Free, generous, and refin'd!
Descend with all thy treasures fraught,
Illumine each bewilder'd thought,
And bless my lab'ring mind.

But first with thy resistless light,
Disperse those phantoms from my sight,
Those mimic shades of thee;
The scholiast's learning, sophist's cant,
The visionary bigot's rant,
The monk's philosophy.

O! let thy powerful charms impart
The patient head, the candid heart,
Devoted to thy sway;
Which no weak passions e'er mislead,
Which still with dauntless steps proceed
Where Reason points the way.

Give me to learn each secret cause;
Let number's, figure's, motion's laws
Reveal'd before me stand;
These to great Nature's scenes apply,
And round the globe, and thro' the sky,
Disclose her working hand.

Next, to thy nobler search resign'd,
The busy, restless, human mind
Thro' ev'ry maze pursue;
Detect Perception where it lies,
Catch the ideas as they rise,
And all their changes view.

Say from what simple springs began
The vast, ambitious thoughts of man,

Which range beyond control;
Which seek Eternity to trace,
Dive thro' th' infinity of space,
And strain to grasp the whole.

Her secret stores let Memory tell,
Bid Fancy quit her fairy cell,
In all her colours drest;
While prompt her sallies to control,
Reason, the judge, recalls the soul
To Truth's severest test.

Then launch thro' Being's wide extent;
Let the fair scale, with just ascent,
And cautious steps, be trod;
And from the dead, corporeal mass,
Thro' each progressive order pass
To Instinct, Reason, God.

There, Science! veil thy daring eye;
Nor dive too deep, nor soar too high,
In that divine abyss;
To Faith content thy beams to lend,
Her hopes t' assure, her steps befriend,
And light her way to bliss.

Then downwards take thy flight agen;
Mix with the policies of men,
And social nature's ties:
The plan, the genius of each state,
Its interest and its pow'rs relate,
Its fortunes and its rise.

Thro' private life pursue thy course,
Trace every action to its source,
And means and motives weigh:
Put tempers, passions in the scale,
Mark what degrees in each prevail,
And fix the doubtful sway.

That last, best effort of thy skill,
To form the life, and rule the will,
Propitious pow'r! impart:
Teach me to cool my passion's fires,
Make me the judge of my desires,
The master of my heart.

Raise me above the vulgar's breath,
Pursuit of fortune, fear of death,
And all in life that's mean.
Still true to reason be my plan,
Still let my action speak the man,
Thro' every various scene.

Hail! queen of manners, light of truth;
Hail! charm of age, and guide of youth;
Sweet refuge of distress:
In business, thou! exact, polite;
Thou giv'st Retirement its delight,
Prosperity its grace.

Of wealth, pow'r, freedom, thou! the cause;
Foundress of order, cities, laws,
Of arts inventress, thou!
Without thee what were human kind?
How vast their wants, their thoughts how blind!
Their joys how mean! how few!

Sun of the soul! thy beams unveil!
Let others spread the daring sail,
On Fortune's faithless sea;
While undeluded, happier I
From the vain tumult timely fly,
And sit in peace with thee.

Mark Akenside 1739

Proof